Administrators in Action

Administrators in Action

VOLUME ONE

BY F. M. G. WILLSON

'The substantial detail . . . gives us the most complete picture we have yet had of the administrative process in Britain. It makes surprisingly compulsive reading.'

The Banker

Administrators in Action

BRITISH CASE STUDIES

VOLUME TWO

BY

GERALD RHODES

LONDON: GEORGE ALLEN & UNWIN LTD
TORONTO: UNIVERSITY OF TORONTO PRESS

FIRST PUBLISHED IN 1965

Published in Canada by the University of Toronto Press

PRINTED IN GREAT BRITAIN
in 11pt Baskerville type
BY UNWIN BROTHERS LIMITED
WOKING AND LONDON

PREFACE

This volume is a successor to the one published in 1961, under the same title, containing five studies written by Professor F. M. G. Willson.

The reasons which led the Royal Institute of Public Administration to embark on this series of case studies in public administration were described in the earlier volume. Briefly, they are to make known more widely the nature of the problem with which public officials are faced, and the methods they employ to resolve them. Studies which fulfil these purposes will be of interest to men of affairs and of value in public service training. In launching this project the Institute received the encouragement and support of the Public Administration Committee of the Joint University Council for Social and Public Administration.

The two studies contained in this second volume have features of special interest. The provision of a better network of roads and motorways is now a matter of great public importance. The study entitled *The Wentworth By-Pass* dealing with the acquisition of land gives an insight into the detailed negotiations which have to be carried out, and the conflicts between private and public interests which have to be settled satisfactorily before the work of construction can begin.

The second study on *New Standards of Accommodation for the Crews of Merchant Ships* is concerned with the application in one particular country of the terms of an international convention. It demonstrates the difficulty of drawing an international convention in terms which are appropriate to the circumstances and customs of different parts of the world, and it provides an illuminating example of the process of consultation in which the British Government engages in the drafting of Regulations.

The Institute wishes to express its sincere gratitude to the Ford Foundation, whose financial support made possible the production of these two volumes of case studies, and to the

Ministry of Transport for allowing the Institute access to its files and giving permission to publish the studies which appear in this volume. Finally, the Institute would like to record its warm appreciation of the valuable work of Mr Gerald Rhodes in developing these studies.

CONTENTS

CASES

I

The Wentworth By-Pass

IMPROVEMENT OF A TRUNK ROAD
A case study of the work of the Ministry of Transport
in land acquisition

CONTENTS

The Wentworth By-Pass

Time-Table of Principal Events

	1939	Trunk road order settled.
21 December	1954	General approval by the Treasury to expenditure on the scheme.
13 February	1955	Divisional Road Engineer requested to approach the Midshire County Council to begin detailed planning.
29 August	1955	Details of the land to be acquired sent by the Divisional Road Engineer to Ministry Headquarters.
11 November	1955	Draft of the side roads order published.
25 February	1956	Lands Branch authorized to begin negotiations for acquisition of land.
11 March	1956	Completion of preliminary work by the Divisional Road Engineer.
8 August	1956	Treasury approval for detailed expenditure.
2 September	1956	Draft of the Compulsory Purchase Order published.
3 September	1956	Arrangements for inviting tenders put in hand.
28 October	1956	Publication of signed Compulsory Purchase Order.
6 November	1956	Tender accepted.
25 November	1956	Road works begun.
December	1957	By-pass opened to traffic.
May	1958	All road works finished.

N.B. The reader may find it helpful to refer to this time-table when reading the detailed narrative.

The Subject of the Case Study

This account will be concerned with the work involved in a section of the Ministry of Transport in the acquisition of land needed for road improvements over a fifteen-mile stretch of a trunk road. For the purposes of the narrative, fictitious names have been used to refer to people and places, but the account of what took place is otherwise completely factual. The general method of exposition adopted has been to follow the progress of the acquisition of a stretch of land from 'Sheepwash Crossroads' to 'Roman Monument', which includes construction of a by-pass at 'Wentworth'. The story will be shown as it appeared to officials in the Headquarters of the Ministry, and as it was dealt with on Headquarters files.

Road building is a matter of considerable public interest and frequently gives rise to discussions in the Press and elsewhere on the subject of whether the progress of road building and road improvement schemes is too slow. One important aspect is the administrative and legal work which is necessary before contractors can gain access to the land to start construction work, and it is part of this work of which a detailed account is given here. The study is therefore particularly concerned with the work done on land acquisition by the Lands Branch of the Highways, Land and Closures Division of the Ministry; this is one of the Divisions of the Highways Administration Group which at the time of the case was in charge of an Under Secretary.

Apart from the public interest in the way this work is organized, this case study brings out a number of issues which concern students of public administration. For example, it shows the way in which work is divided in this Ministry horizontally, according to function, and vertically, according to ranks in the Civil Service hierarchy. It also shows the division of functions and the co-ordination of work between the Ministry and the Treasury Solicitor's Office and the Valuation Office of the Inland Revenue Department, and also between the Headquarters of the Ministry and its Regional representatives, and finally between the Ministry and its agent authorities, the county councils and county borough councils. Other points illustrated are the attitude adopted towards the rights of individual members of the public, and the attempt to standardize internal work by designing a large number of stock forms and letters, in order that work may be delegated to junior levels.

The Lands Branch of the Ministry of Transport

A few words may be said about the organization of that part of the Ministry with which this case study is most concerned. It will be seen from the charts on pages 17–18 that the Highways, Land and Closures Division, of which the Land Branch forms part, was one of five divisions of the Highways Administrative Group, each in charge of an Assistant Secretary.[1] Also shown on the charts are the Highways Engineering Staff who play an important part in the work described in this case; the staff are under the direction of a Chief Engineer, and apart from the Headquarters staff, there are nine offices in England and Wales, each in charge of a Divisional Road Engineer. It is the Divisional Road Engineer who is the Minister's link with the local authorities and who handles all highway matters falling within his area. Within the Highways, Lands and Closures Division, the Lands Branch is the branch responsible for acquiring the land needed for trunk road schemes, whether by agreement or by compulsion. The Branch is also concerned with the management of land which has been acquired, but is not yet needed for trunk road schemes.

At the time when the Wentworth By-Pass was being dealt with (1956), the Lands Branch consisted of two Senior Executive Officers, three Higher Executive Officers, and nine Executive Officers, together with a number of Clerical Officers and Clerical Assistants. The division of the work into sections fell into three main parts. Two sections, under Higher Executive

---

[1] The position shown in the charts is that which existed at the time of the study. Although there has been no major change in the Highways, Land and Closures Division since then, there has been a considerable expansion and reorganization of the remainder of the Highways Administration Group; there are now (1964) 8 divisions in 3 groups, one in charge of an Under Secretary, and two in the joint charge of an Under Secretary and a Deputy Chief Engineer. All these Highway Groups are under the joint charge of a Deputy Secretary and the Director of Highway Engineering.

Officers, dealt with land acquisition, and the third, under the third Higher Executive Officer, was concerned partly with land acquisition work and partly with Compulsory Purchase Orders. The Executive Officers in the Branch were concerned with work on one subject only. One of the acquisition sections contained three Executive Officers and one five. Work on acquisition of land was divided between these two acquisition sections by a division of trunk roads between them.

The work had been so organized that as far as possible the bulk of day-to-day routine operations could be delegated to junior levels, leaving the more senior officers to deal with exceptional cases, changes of policy, preparation of instructions, revision of procedures and difficult correspondence. Stock forms and letters had been prepared to meet the regular requirements of daily work. These had been worked out on the basis of past experience, and the intention was to provide a stock form or letter appropriate for every situation which was regularly encountered.

Because of this method of planning the work it had been possible to delegate the work in this Branch to more junior levels than would otherwise be possible; for example, subsections consisting only of junior staff were expected to carry all normal cases through from beginning to end, submitting only legal documents for signature by senior officers. In an Organization and Methods report, prepared internally in the Department on the work of the Lands Branch, it was said that as a result of this Clerical Officers were able to carry out, and Executive Officers to control, action which, when it occurred in small volume in other parts of the Ministry, engaged the attention of officers at least one and usually two grades higher.

Road Improvement and Land Acquisition

Schemes for the improvement of trunk roads are initiated as a result of surveys of the trunk road system made by the Ministry through its Divisional Road Engineers and the local highway authorities acting as its agents. But the detailed procedures to be followed in making improvements and acquiring land are laid down by Act of Parliament.

The Trunk Roads Act of 1936 made the Minister of Trans-

CHART I

MINISTRY OF TRANSPORT AND CIVIL AVIATION
ORGANIZATION CHART
(HEADQUARTERS (1956))

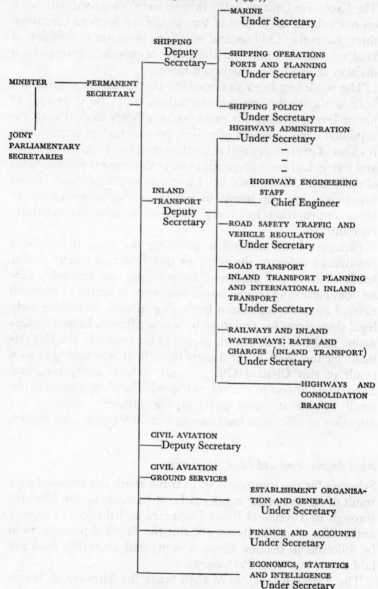

N.B.—Civil Aviation functions are now part of the Ministry of Aviation.

CHART II

HIGHWAYS ADMINISTRATION GROUP

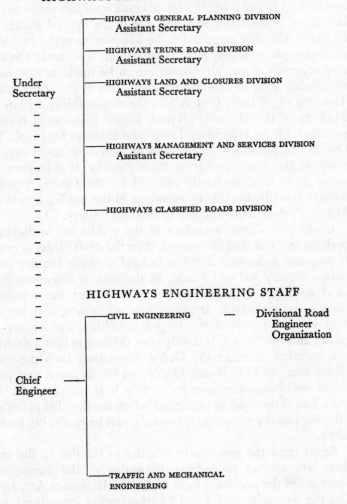

Under
Secretary
— HIGHWAYS GENERAL PLANNING DIVISION
Assistant Secretary

— HIGHWAYS TRUNK ROADS DIVISION
Assistant Secretary

— HIGHWAYS LAND AND CLOSURES DIVISION
Assistant Secretary

— HIGHWAYS MANAGEMENT AND SERVICES DIVISION
Assistant Secretary

— HIGHWAYS CLASSIFIED ROADS DIVISION

HIGHWAYS ENGINEERING STAFF

Chief
Engineer
— CIVIL ENGINEERING — Divisional Road
Engineer
Organization

— TRAFFIC AND MECHANICAL
ENGINEERING

port the highway authority for the roads which constituted the main through routes for traffic. The system was further extended by the Trunk Roads Act of 1946. The procedures to be followed before a new length of trunk road is constructed are laid down in the latter Act, and also in the Special Roads Act of 1949.[1] The first stage is for the Minister to make an Order specifying the new line of the trunk road; a separate Order is also necessary if any alterations are to be made to side roads connecting with or crossing the main line of the trunk road.[2] The making of these Orders was the responsibility within the Ministry of the Highways Trunk Roads Division (a division parallel with the Highways, Lands and Closures Division). The Orders are published locally and objections to them may be made to the Ministry within three months. If objections are made by a local authority affected by the Order, a public inquiry must be held; if by members of the public, it is in the Minister's discretion whether to hold an inquiry.

If objections from members of the public are withdrawn, perhaps as a result of discussions, then the draft Order is made. If not, and a decision is made to hold a public inquiry (or a public inquiry has to be held, in the case of objections from local authorities), a further period of about three months elapses during which arrangements are made, the inquiry held and the report of the Inspector holding the inquiry received and considered. It is only after these steps that a decision can be taken to make the Order. Sometimes both the main Order and the Side Roads Order can be prepared and published simultaneously, but frequently it is necessary for the main line of the road to be settled before the detailed planning, bringing out the effects on side roads, can be profitably undertaken.

Apart from the procedures relating to the line of the road there are similar procedures to authorize the compulsory purchase of the necessary land under the Highways Act, 1959, and the Acquisition of Land (Authorization Procedure) Act,

---

[1] All these are now consolidated with other legislation in the Highways Act, 1959.

[2] For the Statutory requirements see Section 1 (2) and Second Schedule of the 1946 Act (reproduced at Appendix 1) and for side roads Section 14 (1) of the Special Roads Act, 1949. [Now Section 7(2), First Schedule and Section 9 of the Highways Act, 1959.]

1946. These also provide for the preparation and publication of draft Orders (Compulsory Purchase Orders) with the additional point that every person whose land it was intended to acquire, including owners, lessees and most occupiers, receives an individual notice, showing the effect of the draft Order. If objections are received from those with an interest in the land or property and are not withdrawn an inquiry or hearing *must* be held before the Minister reaches his decision unless the objection is only about the amount of compensation payable. Disputes over compensation are for final settlement by the independent Lands Tribunal.

Much of the work of the Lands Branch is semi-legal in character. The Branch works in close collaboration with the Treasury Solicitor who maintains a branch in the Ministry of Transport from whom general legal advice is obtained; in addition, the Treasury Solicitor's Conveyancing Division deals with conveyancing work on behalf of the Ministry and, indeed, many other government departments.[1] At certain stages, as will be shown, negotiations pass out of the hands of the Lands Branch and are taken over by the Treasury Solicitor's Office. An example is the conveyancing work necessary after preliminary negotiations have been completed and permission has been obtained for the contractors to start work on the land. Similarly, at many stages of the work, such as when draft Orders are being prepared, consultation with the Treasury Solicitor's Office is needed.

As well as working closely with the Treasury Solicitor's Office, the staff of the Ministry also call on the services of the Valuation Office of the Inland Revenue Department; valuers of that Department undertake on behalf of the Ministry of Transport the work of valuation of the land to be acquired and negotiate the terms of compensation with the vendors. The work is done by local officers, the District Valuers, of whom there is a network throughout the country. In this case, the District Valuer for the area concerned figures prominently in the various negotiations with the owners of the land which is

---

[1] There is no Ministry of Transport Solicitor as such, despite the fact that there is a good deal of legal work resulting from the Ministry's activities; but whether a department has a separate Solicitor's Branch or relies on the Treasury Solicitor is largely a matter of history and individual circumstance.

being acquired. At the time of the Wentworth Case, all correspondence between officers of the Ministry Headquarters and District Valuers went through the office of the Chief Valuer at the Inland Revenue Headquarters at Somerset House, and thence to the Superintending Valuer of the region which includes the district in question.[1]

PLANNING THE WENTWORTH BY-PASS SCHEME

Engineering and Financial Planning

This project was one of a number of schemes for road improvements, the estimated cost of which was approved by the Treasury on December 21, 1954. An Order covering this line of road had been in force since 1939, when work had been prevented by the Second World War. It was therefore possible for the Ministry to ask the agent authority, the Midshire County Council, through the Divisional Road Engineer, to start making detailed plans. This was done by the despatch of a form (T.R.113A) from the Chief Engineer to the Divisional Road Engineer concerned on February 13, 1955. The form required him to approach the Midshire County Council to obtain detailed drawings and plans, together with an estimate of the cost of the work, and 'reference schedules' with details of the land to be acquired including ownership and occupancies. The cost as estimated at this stage at Headquarters was £131,000.

An officer of the Midshire County Council signed and returned to the Divisional Road Engineer another form (T.R.113B) accepting the Minister's invitation for the preparation of the scheme. The Divisional Road Engineer then consulted various public authorities whose interests were affected including the Regional Land Commissioner of the Ministry of Agriculture, Fisheries and Food, the Local River Catchment Board and the Drainage Board. He also examined various technical problems such as whether it would be necessary to demolish any habitable property, or whether the road was situated in an area where minerals had been or were

---

[1] The normal procedure now is for correspondence to go direct from the Ministry to the Superintending Valuer and thence to the District Valuer (and vice versa).

being worked. Some of these consultations, and the examination of the technical problems, may have begun before the form T.R.113B was received back from the Midshire County Council. Having completed this work, the Divisional Road Engineer informed the Highways (Trunk Roads) Division of the Ministry on March 11, 1956. This notification too was done by means of a form (T.R.113C) which gives details of the various technical points and consultations. It will be noticed that this was just over one year from the date on which the Divisional Road Engineer had been requested to begin action.

The form (T.R.113C) also serves to record approval within the Ministry of the detailed expenditure on the scheme. This was not done until August 8, 1956, as there was much discussion with the Treasury before approval was given.

In order to speed up the work of negotiating the acquisition of land, the 'reference schedules' and plans showing the precise details of land to be acquired had already been sent to the Highways (Trunk Roads) Division on August 29, 1955 by the Divisional Road Engineer before the detailed form (T.R.113C) was ready. They were then passed by the Highways (Trunk Roads) Division to the Lands Branch on February 25, 1956. This six months' interval was caused by the need to wait until the objection period in connection with the making of the Side Roads Order had expired (see page 26 below) and also for the Treasury approval for the expenditure on land and compensation.

In connection with the second of these two items, the Divisional Road Engineer had sent to the Highways (Trunk Roads) Division on September 13, 1955 a separate estimate of the cost of land and of compensation for disturbance of business and of restoration of damage to property. This last is known as 'accommodation works' and includes such matters as replacing fences, ditches, drains, walls and so on. The estimated cost for land and compensation was £27,500 (excluding 'accommodation works'). Treasury approval for this expenditure on land and compensation had to be obtained before the Lands Branch could be authorized by the Highways (Trunk Roads) Division to start their negotiations; this approval was obtained on December 10, 1955.

Nevertheless, even with these delays the Lands Branch were

able to request the District Valuer to start negotiations for acquiring the necessary land before final estimates of costs for the work as a whole were settled and agreed with the Treasury on August 8, 1956. After that date the Highways (Trunk Roads) Division prepared a final programme for the Lands Branch and the Divisional Road Engineer to work to (on form T.R.113D). This was signed on September 3, 1956, by an officer of the rank of Higher Executive Officer in the Highways (Trunk Roads) Division. The Lands Branch were now asked to obtain entry on to the land by January 3, 1957. This was 5½ months later than the original target date of July 15th, which could not be met (see page 34).

The Divisional Road Engineer was asked to issue form T.R.113E to the agent authority, in this case the Midshire County Council, inviting them to undertake the work of road improvement either by direct labour or by putting it out to tender. The form states:

> The Minister is proceeding to acquire the land necessary for the road works and your attention is particularly directed to the need for keeping in touch with the Divisional Road Engineer to ascertain the progress of the land acquisition in order to ensure so far as is practicable that there is no undue delay between the date of inviting tenders and the date of giving contractors entry to the site.

Also on September 3, 1956, the Highways (Trunk Roads) Division issued another form (T.R.113F) signed by a Higher Executive Officer, asking the Divisional Road Engineer to authorize the Midshire County Council to invite tenders for the road works. Tenders were submitted by the agent authority to the Divisional Road Engineer, who in turn sent them to Headquarters to Highways (Management and Services) Division where they were examined so that the lowest satisfactory tender could be accepted. On November 6, 1956, the Divisional Road Engineer was informed by the issue of form T.R.113H, signed by an Executive Officer in the Highways (Trunk Roads) Division, of the tender to be accepted. With this form T.R.113H went a note saying that entry to a number of plots of land had been secured. This was based on information from the Lands Branch sent to him by a Higher

Executive Officer by means of a stock form dated November 5, 1956.

Official authorization was given to the Midshire County Council on November 12th, to accept the tender and carry out the works; the road work began on November 25, 1956, and the By-Pass was opened to traffic in December 1957. The whole of the road work was finished by May 1958.

From this account of the planning work, it will be seen that the activities of estimating costs, obtaining Treasury approval, authorizing expenditure and arranging for the work to be done, either by the agent authority's own labour or by contractors, are closely linked with the steps needed to secure entry by the labour force on to the land. But as well as co-ordinating all these activities, it was also necessary for all concerned to bear in mind the need for legal authority and the next section will deal with this aspect.

Legal Authority: Trunk Road and Side Roads Order

As has been said above, two Orders were needed, a Trunk Road Order and a Side Roads Order. Before any detailed planning of the scheme could be undertaken on the basis of the broad general plan, the line of the road had to be established by a Trunk Road Order.

The Order for the Wentworth By-Pass, as was stated earlier, had been made in 1939 by means of a Statutory Rule and Order under the Trunk Roads Act, 1936. In accordance with Section 1 of that Act, the local county council was informed of the Minister's intention to construct the By-Pass in a letter signed by an Assistant Secretary and dated January 19, 1938. At the same time, although this was not required by the Act, the Ministry arranged for publication of a notice of the intention in two local newspapers on April 10, 1938, and for notices to be displayed in the area, and a copy of the draft Order and a plan to be deposited at the council's offices for inspection by members of the public. The notices invited members of the public, if they wished, to make any representations in writing to Ministry Headquarters before May 2, 1938. A letter was also sent to the local Catchment Board, as bridges might be affected.

It will be noticed that by informing the public of what was intended the Ministry followed a procedure which later came into force under the Trunk Roads Act of 1946. A public inquiry was held, and after considering representations, the Minister decided that the Order providing for the By-Pass to be constructed should, in fact, be made.

When the scheme was again brought forward in December 1954, the Trunk Road Order was therefore in force, but it was necessary for a Side Roads Order to be made. Detailed plans showing the proposed alterations to side roads were sent to the Chief Engineer's Division at Headquarters on April 30, 1955, signed by a Senior Engineer on behalf of the Divisional Road Engineer for the Midshire Division. On June 13, 1955, a member of the Chief Engineer's staff at Headquarters counter-signed these plans and sent them to the Orders Section of the Highways (Trunk Roads) Division for preparation of the Side Roads Order.

After a draft Order had been prepared and checked by the Divisional Road Engineer, a notice of the preparation of the draft Order was signed by the Assistant Secretary in charge of the Highways (Trunk Roads) Division on November 11, 1955 and a copy sent to the Divisional Road Engineer for information. On the same day, this notice of the intention to make the Order and a copy of the draft Order were sent to the Midshire County Council to be displayed for the information of the public.

At the same time the following government departments were informed: the Post Office Telecommunications Department, the Ministry of Agriculture, Fisheries and Food, the Ministry of Fuel and Power and the Ministry of Housing and Local Government. This was because of the possible effect of the work on cables, the grid, land development and so on. In fact, an electricity pole had to be re-sited and a pipe lowered as a result of the work. A three months' objection period was allowed, running from November 15, 1955. A number of objections were received at the Ministry's Headquarters, but these related to the making of the By-Pass itself and not to the effect on side roads. Since the making of the By-Pass had been legally authorized by the Statutory Rule and Order of 1939 the objections were not legally relevant. The Orders Section replied to them by explaining the need for the improvement in the national interest and pointing out that unless a By-Pass were made, the road through the village would have to be widened with extensive demolition of property.

The Side Roads Order was sealed on April 14, 1956, and signed by an Under Secretary of the Ministry. Copies of the final Order were sent to the Midshire County Council and a notice was published in the *London Gazette* on May 21, 1956.

Legal Authority: Compulsory Purchase Order

On February 25, 1956, the Highways (Trunk Roads) Division were able, at the expiration of the objection period, to instruct the Lands Branch to begin work on land acquisition. For this purpose, they passed to them the 'reference schedules' and plans (see page 23 above). These were checked by the Acquisition Section concerned who then sent copies to the Office of the Chief Valuer to open negotiations with the owners.

On March 16, 1956, the Higher Executive Officer in charge of the Acquisition Section responsible for this trunk road[1] notified the Executive Officer in charge of the Compulsory Purchase Order Section of the Lands Branch that a Compulsory Purchase Order should be made covering the land to be acquired, with the exception of that owned by the Crown Estate Commissioners. The Order is prepared in case it is needed while negotiations are in progress to secure voluntary agreement for plots of land to be sold.[2]

On March 25th the Executive Officer in the Compulsory Purchase Order Section wrote to the Divisional Road Engineer asking him to prepare a plan to be attached to the Order, showing the land to be included in it. At the same time he sent a stock letter to the Clerk of the Midshire County Council asking him if he would arrange for a copy of the draft Order and plan when prepared to be deposited at the Council's offices for inspection by the public. In April and May 1956

---

[1] He will be referred to as 'H.E.O.(A.S.)' for short in future. Similarly, his Executive Officer will be referred to as 'E.O.(A.S.)'.

[2] A 'plot' in the technical sense used by the Ministry refers to a piece of land with a single owner and a single occupier. Two adjoining pieces of land with a single owner but two different occupiers would constitute two plots as they would if they had different owners but a single occupier.

several minutes were exchanged between the E.O. and the Divisional Road Engineer's office in order to clear up detailed points relating to ownership of individual plots, and by the end of June 1956 it was possible for the Compulsory Purchase Order Section to prepare a draft Compulsory Purchase Order. Copies of this were sent by the E.O. to the Treasury Solicitor's Office on June 24, 1956, to the Divisional Road Engineer and to the Chief Valuer at Somerset House, on the same date, for their observations.

All seemed to be going smoothly, and on July 8th the District Valuer for the Midshire District reported that in all but five cases, permits to enter had been received (a copy of this letter is on page 33). This information was sent by the E.O. in the Compulsory Purchase Order Section to one of the Clerical Officers in the Acquisition Section concerned with this scheme.

After one or two more points concerning ownership of plots had been cleared up by an exchange of further minutes between the E.O. and the Divisional Road Engineer, it was possible to publish the draft Compulsory Purchase Order. A copy was sent to the Parliamentary Branch to arrange for publication in a local newspaper. Again a stock form was used, signed by the E.O. on August 22, 1956. (A copy of the Compulsory Purchase Order minus the Schedule and Plan, is attached as Appendix 2.)

On September 1, 1956 a notice of the preparation of the draft Compulsory Purchase Order was sent to all the owners, lessees and occupiers of the plots which would be affected, with a covering letter, drawing attention to the fact that any objections to the draft Compulsory Purchase Order must be made in writing by September 27th, and that if objections were made (and not withdrawn) a public inquiry or other hearing would be held. On August 29, 1956 the E.O. informed the E.O.(A.S.) by the use of a stock form that the draft Compulsory Purchase Order would be published on September 2, 1956 and that the objection period would expire on September 27, 1956. On September 1st, the E.O. also sent copies of the draft Compulsory Purchase Order to the Divisional Road Engineer for Midshire and to the Chief Valuer at Somerset House. Copies were also deposited in one of the Ministry's Headquarter Offices in

London for inspection by the public and the Enquiry Officers were instructed that callers should be shown the draft Order.

Although it looked as if there would be a settlement for sale by agreement in all cases, since no objections had been received, on October 3rd, the E.O. asked the E.O.(A.S.) to say whether there had been any difficulties in negotiations. One of the Clerical Officers in the Acquisition Section replied on October 7th that there had so far been no difficulties, and the E.O. therefore on October 8th sent the Order for signature to the Assistant Secretary of the Highways, Land and Closures Division. He signed it on October 10, 1956. It was then forwarded to the Parliamentary Branch to be kept in safe custody.

On October 22nd, the E.O. sent a stock form of letter to the Clerk of the Midshire County Council with a copy of the final Order, which he asked him to arrange to be displayed to the public for a period of six weeks. During this period representations could be made to the High Court questioning its legal validity. In view of the possible interest of the National Coal Board, as shown in Article 2, the E.O. also sent a copy to them. He sent further copies to the E.O.(A.S.), on October 22nd and to the Divisional Road Engineer, the Chief Valuer, and the Secretary of the Department of Inland Revenue on October 27, 1956. The Order became operative on October 28th. A copy was placed in one of the Ministry's London offices for inspection by the public for six weeks from October 28 to December 10, 1956, and a notice was included in a local newspaper on October 28, 1956. As with the draft Order, letters were sent to each owner, lessee or occupier, together with a copy of a notice of the making of the Order and of the Order itself.

This concludes the work connected with ensuring that all the requirements of the Acts governing the making of the road improvements and the compulsory purchase of the land had been complied with.

OBTAINING THE LAND

Sheepwash Cross Roads to Roman Monument

We come now to the central part of the story, the account of the detailed work which went into the acquisition of the plots of land needed over the 15-mile stretch of land from Sheepwash Cross Roads to Roman Monument. In order to make the story as a whole clear, an outline will first be given of the main work undertaken in the Lands Branch, with some reference to the work undertaken in connection with three sets of individual negotiations, that is, Farmer Bishop's cowsheds, re-housing Mrs Waters, and the lands belonging to the Crown. The outline will be followed by a step by step account of the work involved in these three sets of individual negotiations, largely told in the form of letters, minutes and reports reproduced, with the necessary disguise, from the Ministry's files.

The signal for the Acquisition Section of the Lands Branch, which was responsible for this trunk road, to start arrangements for the acquisition of land, was a minute dated February 25, 1956, to which reference has already been made (see page 27) from an Executive Officer in the Highways (Trunk Roads) Division. This informed the H.E.O.(A.S.) that there had been no objection to the Side Roads Order and that he should start negotiations for land acquisition and try to obtain permission from all holders of the plots to be sold for contractors to enter by July 15, 1956. The reference schedules accompanying this minute as will be remembered, had been sent by the Divisional Road Engineer on August 29, 1955. They described in detail each plot of land and its ownership.

A note was attached to the reference schedules pointing out that at the time when the 1939 Statutory Rule and Order had been made, an undertaking had been given to the farmer, James Bishop, that his cowsheds would be rebuilt. The new line of the road would place his existing cowsheds on the wrong side so that four times a day his cattle would have to cross the main road, constituting a danger both to themselves and to the traffic. A note was also attached saying that it might be necessary to re-house Mrs Waters, as her cottage might have to be demolished to make way for a roundabout.

The reference schedules were examined by a Clerical Officer in the Acquisition Section, who completed an analysis, using a stock form (LB 1). This form was submitted with comments on another stock form (LB 2) to the E.O.(A.S.).

The local negotiations with plotholders to secure their agreement for workmen to enter on their land by the target

date, were to be undertaken as normally by the local District
Valuer. The E.O. therefore sent the reference plan showing the
land needed, and the reference schedule (on form TR 138) to
the Chief Valuer at Somerset House on March 9, 1956, using
another stock letter (LB 3) which follows:

Chief Valuer,
East Wing,   LB.3.
Somerset House.

X10 Trunk Road
*Scheme Construction of second carriageway from Sheepwash Cross Roads to
Roman Monument*

It is now possible to ask you to arrange for negotiations to be
opened for the land required in connection with the above-
mentioned scheme. I therefore enclose:

(1) Two copies of the Reference Plan ST.
(2) Two copies of the Reference Schedule.

Your attention is drawn to the following points:

(a) Our Divisional Road Engineer has been instructed to forward
Plot plans direct to the District Valuer and at the same time to
advise him as to the type of accommodation works and fencing it
is proposed to adopt.

(b) It is proposed to proceed with a Draft Compulsory Purchase
Order as respects this scheme concurrently with the District
Valuer's negotiations and a draft Order will be submitted to you
for observations in due course. It is thought that there is no need
for the District Valuer to refer to the fact that a Compulsory
Purchase Order is being drafted as each person scheduled to the
Order will receive a suitable letter with Notice of the preparation
of the Order, informing him that the Order is without prejudice
to any provisional settlement reached or under negotiation with
the District Valuer. It is requested that the District Valuer may
notify the Department as early as possible of the plots in respect of
which he desires that Notice to Treat should be served.

(c) *Minerals.* The general policy of the Minister is not to purchase
minerals other than surface minerals and those necessary to be
dug or carried away in the course of the road construction or
improvement. He wishes, however, to take whatever right of
support the Vendor of the surface land has and can give (prefer-
ably expressed in terms of the Mining Code) or of compensation
for subsidence. The Mining Code would be applied to all ac-
quisitions of land following the making of a C.P.O. The Minister
has no power to acquire coal. In a non-mining area, however,

where the Vendor owns the sub-soil and does not wish to reserve the minerals, the acquisition will include them except coal.

(d) Entry is required by 15th July 1956 and the District Valuer should be requested to secure entry by this date or, if this proves impossible, to notify this Office without delay.

In order that the various steps towards the commencement of works may proceed to plan it is desired to have a report by 15th June 1956 at the latest saying whether or not the District Valuer anticipates being able to arrange for entry on the date first specified and in the negative cases, whether he recommend service of Notice to Treat and in respect of which plots.

(4) Application has been made to the Tithe Redemption Commission for particulars of the respective Tithe Annuities in order that informal apportionments can be assessed. Details will be forwarded as soon as received.

At the same time, on March 9, 1956, the E.O.(A.S.) wrote to the Divisional Road Engineer for the Midshire Division, informing him that the Chief Valuer had been asked to arrange for the District Valuer to open negotiations, and asking him to supply the local District Valuer with individual plans illustrating each owner's or lessee's plot or group of plots. This he did, and on April 1, 1956 sent copies of these to Lands Branch. The E.O.(A.S.) also asked the Divisional Road Engineer to inform the District Valuer what accommodation works, that is fencing, replacing walls and ditches etc., the Divisional Road Engineer proposed to carry out for each plot. Once again a stock letter was used.

On March 15, 1956, the E.O.(A.S.) wrote to the Crown Estate Commissioners, who owned several of the plots, and asked them if they would agree that the valuation of the land for purposes of sale by the Commissioners to the Ministry should, as normally, be undertaken by the Department of Inland Revenue.

The work of obtaining permission to enter was now in the hands of the District Valuer. As he obtained signatures from owners, tenants and lessees, he sent them to the Chief Valuer, who in turn passed them to the Lands Branch. A simple form of permission was used. By June 14th, one month before the target date for entry, the District Valuer reported the position regarding permission to enter to the Chief Valuer, who passed on his letter to the Lands Branch, as requested in the letter LB3 already quoted.

The following is an extract from his letter dated June 14, 1956:

> ... the position with regard to permission to enter the various plots is as follows:
>
> Plots 1, 2, 4 and 5 have presumably already been dealt with direct (Crown lands). Only four permissions, apart from these, have been obtained. It is expected that most of the remainder will be obtained within the next week or so; there may, however, be difficulty about plot 16 (tenancy interest) where a petrol filling station is involved, and also plots Nos. 13, 14, 16, 17, 18 and 19 (no reply so far from freeholders). Also plots Nos. 11, 14, 15 and 19, no reply from tenants. This latter group involves reinstatement of a dwelling-house. Every endeavour will be made, however, to obtain all the permits within the shortest possible time and it is not yet possible to state whether compulsory powers will be needed with regard to the last-named group.

A draft Compulsory Purchase Order had been sent to the Chief Valuer in June 1956 and he had forwarded it to the District Valuer (see page 28 above). By July 8th the District Valuer was able to be much more hopeful as is shown by his letter to the Chief Valuer of that date, which the Chief Valuer sent to the Lands Branch:

> With reference to your memo dated 29th June last, one copy each of the draft Compulsory Purchase Order, draft schedule and plan is returned herewith, suitably amended to conform to the latest alterations. I have no objection to the inclusion in the Order of any of the interests shown in the draft schedule, provided that this office is informed before Notices to Treat are served. However you may not consider this procedure necessary in view of the position regarding Permits to Enter, which is as follows:
>
> *Plot 5 Tenant's interest.* Permit promised shortly.
>
> *Plots 11 and 11a.* Permits to enter promised shortly by the Freeholders.
>
> *Plot 12.* Permit to enter promised shortly (Freehold interest).
>
> *Plot 20.* Discussions with the Planning Authorities are in progress with the freeholders with regard to car parking arrangements. Although these are expected to result in agreement shortly, no Permit to Enter will be forthcoming until then.

Plot 16. The lessees are hoping to find alternative premises nearby for their petrol filling station, but are unwilling to give entry at this stage.

Permits in all other cases have been received and forwarded to you.

At this point, the E.O.(A.S.) informed the Treasury Solicitor's Conveyancing Division of the state of progress on a stock form (LB5), with copies of the reference schedule and plan.

It was not possible for work to start on the original target date, as sufficient agreements to enter had not been obtained. The E.O. therefore informed the Highways (Trunk Roads) Division of this in a minute dated August 25, 1956, and asked for a new target date. The Highways (Trunk Roads) Division issued a time-table for work (on form T.R.113D), containing the new target date of January 3, 1957. One difficulty which held up the progress of the work was the problem of rehousing a tenant Mrs Waters. This story is told in 'Rehousing a Plotholder'.

During the period while efforts were being made to get agreement to enter from all the plotholders, there had also been an interchange of correspondence between the E.O.(A.S.) and the Crown Estate Commissioners to try to secure agreement on the form of a joint submission to the Inland Revenue Valuation Office in connection with the land to be purchased by the Ministry from the Commissioners. This story is also told in detail later in 'Acquisition of Crown Estate Land'.

On October 22, 1956 the E.O. of the Compulsory Purchase Order Section informed the E.O.(A.S.) that the Compulsory Purchase Order had been sealed on October 10, 1956 and asked her to send a copy to the Treasury Solicitor's Conveyancing Division, which she did on October 23rd. Meanwhile the Divisional Road Engineer was becoming anxious to arrange with the County Surveyor for the contractor to be instructed to make an effective start on the work before the end of November 1956. He wrote to the Lands Branch on October 28, 1956 asking that entry should be secured on as many of the plots as possible.

Fortunately for the Ministry, the problem of rehousing Mrs Waters had been overcome, as a property belonging to the Ministry was about to become vacant, and she had agreed to

34

accept the tenancy of this. A letter of October 29th from the Divisional Road Engineer informed the Lands Branch of this development.

On November 5th, the H.E.O.(A.S.), notified the Highways (Trunk Roads) Division of the number of plots (that is the great majority) on which agreement to enter had been secured, once again using a stock form, and the Highways (Trunk Roads) Division were therefore able to issue the form T.R.113H, notifying the Divisional Road Engineer of the tender to be accepted. This form T.R.113H together with the list of plots on which entry could be made was sent to the Divisional Road Engineer on November 5, 1956 (see page 24 above).

The final agreements for permission to enter came in one by one to the Lands Branch via the Chief Valuer as the latter received them from the District Valuer, and on December 3rd and December 5th the Highways (Trunk Roads) Division were notified of further plots where permission had been obtained; the last notification that entry could be made on to the land where Mrs Waters' cottage was to be demolished was sent to the Highways (Trunk Roads) Division for transmission to the Divisional Road Engineer on March 30, 1957. Mrs Waters had agreed to move from her old cottage not later than March 28, 1957. Work on the site had begun on November 25, 1956, the By-Pass was opened to traffic in December 1957, and the remaining stretch of road in May 1958.

Payment of Compensation

Although the vital task from the point of view of the Ministry was for permission to be obtained from the plotholders for the contractors to enter on their land and start work, from the plotholders' point of view the essential thing was that they should get their money as quickly as possible. To illustrate the work involved in this, accounts will now be given of two settlements where there were no difficulties. Two methods of settlement are possible, by conveyance and by 'shortened procedure'; the latter is a method of avoiding the trouble and expense of a deed of conveyance where the amount of the purchase money and compensation is £100 or less.[1] The vendor gives permission

---

[1] The amount has now been raised to £500.

for the use of the land and agrees to convey it to the purchaser if required by him to do so.

The conveyance procedure was used in the case of Mr Bourne, since the District Valuer assessed the amount of purchase money and compensation at £120. On June 11,1956 the District Valuer signed his report and sent it to the Chief Valuer, who counter-signed it on June 16, 1956 and sent it to the Ministry's Land Branch. The District Valuer's report was then examined by a Clerical Officer in the Acquisition Section, who completed an analysis of points using a stock form (LB 7A).

One of the points on which the District Valuer's report commented was the accommodation works which the Ministry were to undertake on Mr Bourne's behalf. In order to ensure that the description of these exactly corresponded with the intentions of the Divisional Road Engineer, the wording was agreed with him in the form of a draft schedule to be included as part of the formal conveyance, which read as follows:

DRAFT SCHEDULE
CONDITIONS AND STIPULATIONS

The Minister at his own expense and with all convenient and reasonable speed after the purchase or improvement of the said road on the said land has been commenced shall make the undermentioned works for the accommodation of the adjoining land of the vendor videlicet:

(i) At the Vendor's request sufficiently fence the said land during the execution of the works so as to prevent the straying of stock from the adjoining land of the Vendor.

(ii) Plant upon the easterly side of so much of the said adjoining land of the Vendor as abuts the said land a quick hedge and erect upon the westerly side of the said hedge a concrete post and 5-strand wire fence.

(iii) Provide two access gaps on the new boundary in similar positions to the existing gaps.

(iv) Make good the land drainage system which may be disturbed during the progress of the work and connect where necessary to the new roadside ditch.

So soon as the said hedge is planted, fence erected and access gaps set back on the said adjoining land, the same shall become the property of the Vendor and the Minister shall not thereafter be responsible for their maintenance except that the Minister shall maintain the said hedge for a period of five years from the date of planting.

After making sure that there were no unusual features about the case, which, in accordance with the standard procedure was undertaken by a Clerical Officer, the E.O.(A.S.) on August 6, 1956, recommended to the H.E.O., that the Treasury Solicitor's Conveyancing Division should be asked to prepare the form of conveyance, and on the same date the H.E.O. sent a form (LB 11) with details of Mr Bourne's case to the Conveyancing Division. On December 4th, the Treasury Solicitor's Conveyancing Division sent a draft conveyance to the Lands Branch for checking. One point raised in a letter of December 21, 1956 to the Treasury Solicitor's Conveyancing Division was that as the Compulsory Purchase Order had meanwhile been made, it might be mentioned in the conveyance. On January 23, 1957 the Treasury Solicitor's Conveyancing Division asked the Lands Branch for a payable order for the sum of £120, together with surveyor's fee of £14 14s and the vendor's solicitor's costs of £8 8s od, totalling £143 2s od, and the Finance Division supplied this to the Conveyancing Division on February 18th. The Treasury Solicitor's Office arranged for the signing and witnessing of the conveyance, which was dated February 27, 1957, and on March 3rd sent the original copy to the Parliamentary Branch for sealing on behalf of the Minister.

From the point of view of Mr Bourne, all was well settled, but the Lands Branch followed up the settlement by sending to the Divisional Road Engineer a copy of the schedule as it appeared in the conveyance, describing the accommodation works to be carried out. This was done by means of a stock form, which was signed by the E.O.(A.S.) on March 28, 1957. The form included a request for the Divisional Road Engineer to notify the Lands Branch when the accommodation works had been completed, and also an additional copy of the description of these works was enclosed for the Divisional Road Engineer to transmit to the Midshire County Council. On the same date, March 28th, the E.O. notified the Chief Inspector of Taxes, Public Departments, at Cardiff, of the change of ownership of this land,[1] and also notified the Tithe Redemption Commission.

An example of the shortened procedure was the case of Mrs Jones' plot. In his report, dated October 28, 1956, the District Valuer gave an assessment of £100 for purchase price and compensation. The report was countersigned by the Chief Valuer on October 30, 1956. The District Valuer in his report said that the vendor had agreed to sign a form of receipt and undertaking which would take the place of a conveyance. On November 15th, the E.O.(A.S.) wrote, using a stock form, to the Divisional Road Engineer setting out a description of the accommodation works, which were very similar to those to be undertaken for Mr Bourne, and on November 21, 1956, the Divisional Road Engineer replied saying that the wording clearly indicated his intentions. A form of 'Receipt and Undertaking (Shortened Procedure)' was prepared by the completion in the Lands Branch by a Clerical Officer of a stock form.

On December 9, 1956, the E.O. sent two copies of this draft form and copies of a plan of the land to the vendor's solicitors, asking them to arrange for their client to sign the form and plan, have the signatures witnessed and return the forms and plans for signature on behalf of the Minister. The solicitors replied on December 13, 1956, returning the signed forms and plans. The E.O. on December 21st sent the form of Receipt and Undertaking (Shortened Procedure) to the Treasury Solicitor's Conveyancing Division for registration of land charge. On the same day, December 21st, she wrote to the vendor's solicitors enclosing a payable order for £115 15s 0d, which covered the agreed price of £100, plus surveyor's fees of £10 10s 0d, and solicitor's costs of £5 5s 0d.

Notification that the land charge had been registered came to the Lands Branch from the Treasury Solicitor's Conveyancing Division on January 13, 1957, and they returned the Receipt and Undertaking at the same time. Once again, as in the case of Mr Bourne, the E.O. notified the Chief Inspector of Taxes, Public Departments, on February 17, 1957, and also

[1] The object of doing this is to ensure that all changes in Income Tax charges affecting land and property in which government departments have an interest are channelled through a central point; the Chief Inspector at Cardiff has the duty of passing on the Ministry's notifications to the appropriate local Inspector of Taxes.

on the same date sent a stock letter to the Divisional Road Engineer reminding him of the accommodation works to be undertaken and asking him to inform the Lands Branch when they were completed. On the same date, she sent the Receipt and Undertaking to the Parliamentary Branch for safe custody.

COWSHEDS ON THE WRONG SIDE OF THE ROAD

Mr Bishop's Request

The acquisition of Mr Bourne's and Mrs Jones's plots of land was straightforward, but in the case of Mr James Bishop, there were complications. When the scheme was first mooted in 1938, it was found that the alteration in the line of the road would pass through Mr Bishop's farmlands, separating his fields for grazing from his cowsheds. It was therefore provisionally agreed at that time that when the road improvements were made, new cowsheds would be built for him, and possibly an undercreep for cattle and farm machinery to pass under the new road. In 1955, when the scheme was again revived, this problem still remained to be solved. A note of the original discussions had been made in Ministry Headquarters when the scheme was being considered in 1938.

The problem was brought to the attention of the Lands Branch by a telephone call from the Divisional Road Engineer in May 1956. A note of this conversation and a request for a decision about whether the Ministry should rebuild the cowsheds or not, was made by the H.E.O.(A.S.), who sought the advice of a Higher Executive Officer in the Highways (Trunk Roads) Division, in the following terms on May 9, 1956:

> Mr A. Phillips, Divisional Road Engineer, Midshire, phoned me last week about this scheme which incorporates Wentworth By-Pass. He referred me to the précis of representations of 1st November 1939 and the 'undertaking' opposite the name of Mr Bishop who is, I understand, the owner-occupier of plot 8 and one of the trustees who own plot 8a, which he also tenants in this scheme (entry permission granted). Mr Phillips informs me that the District Valuer in his negotiations has not been asked to honour any undertaking but that the question of rebuilding the

cowsheds, but *not* constructing a cattle-creep, has come up because the District Valuer, having increased his compensation figure as far as he can, still cannot offer enough to allow Mr Bishop sufficient for him to rebuild the cowsheds. Mr Phillips says that the possibility of a grant from Ministry of Agriculture was investigated but this fell through because ownership of the holding is split and the part owned is not big enough to qualify.

Mr Phillips estimates that the cost of rebuilding the cowsheds would be £6,500 and the cost of the cattle creep from £8,000 to £12,000 or £15,000. The District Valuer, Mr Phillips says, would take into account the work done in rebuilding the cowsheds in assessing compensation. (I suppose this would mean no monetary payment whatsoever!) The point is whether we agree to rebuild the cowshed and I think that your Division has to make a decision. There seem to me to be a few material points to mention, viz.:

(i) The nearest approach to an undertaking is on the attached file in para 3 of the Divisional Road Engineer's minute of 25th July 1939 (flagged Y).

(ii) There may, however, be some more definite understanding than this perhaps on file PB2/182 or on the recent 14(1) Orders file, although if there is, it is surprising that Mr Bishop has not raised the matter on that basis.

(iii) To rebuild the cowsheds, in terms of cash, exceeds the compensation the District Valuer can offer, but there is the nuisance to traffic by cattle to consider.

Will you please consider the problem raised by Mr Phillips. I take it you will let him know what decision is reached, and, if so, I should like a copy of your letter for this file.

This H.E.O., in his turn, consulted his Principal, in the following minute of May 12th:

There is no more information available apparently to supplement what the H.E.O. has said about replacing the cowsheds and constructing a cattle creep. I think it is clear from the précis of representations dated 1/6/40 on the attached file that we are morally committed. In view, however, of what is said above, it seems that we could confine ourselves to rebuilding the cowsheds. I think, however, the Divisional Road Engineer should give a firm recommendation, and if you agree that in the circumstances we should honour our 1939 undertaking, I will minute DRE accordingly.

Having secured the Principal's agreement, the H.E.O. then

informed the E.O.(A.S.) of the action taken. On May 20, 1956 the Divisional Road Engineer sent a report to the Highways (Trunk Roads) Division on the current state of affairs with regard to these inconveniently placed cowsheds. The following extracts from his report show the main points he made:

When the Wentworth By-Pass Order was under consideration in 1939, the main objection of any importance was made by a Mr James Bishop who was Vice-Chairman of the Rural District Council and farmed a considerable area of land on both sides of the proposed By-Pass.

His objection was on grounds of severance and the danger and inconvenience of herds of cows crossing the trunk road four times per day. A report was submitted from this office to the Deputy Chief Engineer on 26th January, 1939.

It was suggested that new cowsheds be built on the east side of the By-Pass.

A minute was received from (Headquarters) . . . saying 'The cowsheds will be rebuilt on a site adjoining the east side of the By-Pass and a cattle creep will be constructed.'

According to the papers on my file, the District Valuer had at the time been informed that there had been discussions with Mr Bishop about the provision of new cowsheds and a cattle creep, and as regards the former, the District Valuer was asked to include in his estimate of the cost of acquisition for their provision.

In the present negotiations, the District Valuer has been approached about the provision of cowsheds, with milking equipment, on the east side of the By-Pass for the same Mr James Bishop.

. . . The District Valuer is in some difficulty in that whilst he has gone as far as he possibly can over the question of compensation this is insufficient to meet the cost of the construction of new buildings on the east side of the By-Pass (I should mention that the existing buildings while quite useable would not stand removal and re-erection) . . .

I understand that the cost of suitable buildings and equipment is likely to be in the region of £6,500.

. . . The District Valuer feels that if we treat the provision of new buildings as accommodation works that will resolve his difficulties. He will of course take this into account in the compensation.

. . . As far as I can see the cattle creep would serve no purpose now, if there are cowsheds for Mr Bishop on the east side as well

41

as the west side. . . . I gather that the matter of the cattle creep is unlikely to be pressed if the cowsheds are agreed.

So far as the cattle sheds are concerned this is reasonable in view of the severance and the public safety aspect of cattle having to cross the fast and heavily trafficked By-Pass daily for milking, and I recommend that it be agreed that their provision be treated as accommodation works.

It will be appreciated if this matter could be dealt with quickly, please, so that the building can be undertaken and completed concurrently with the roadworks.

On June 21st the H.E.O. in the Division replied to the request from the Divisional Road Engineer saying that the pre-war undertaking was that the Ministry would rebuild the cowsheds on the other side of the road but not provide new buildings or equipment; but the Division would agree to the cost of new buildings, after deducting the contribution expected from the Ministry of Agriculture.

This decision followed an exchange of minutes between the Principal in the Highways (Trunk Roads) Division, and the Finance Division, in which the former explained the pre-war undertaking and said that he had heard by telephone from the Divisional Road Engineer that the Ministry of Agriculture would provide a grant amounting to one-third of the cost of the new cowsheds. The Finance Division had agreed that the Ministry should pay the remaining two-thirds.

However, on October 21st the Divisional Road Engineer reported disappointing news, in the following minute to the Highways (Trunk Roads) Division:

X10 Trunk Road
improvement from Sheepwash Cross to Roman Monument,
Wentworth By-Pass, Mr James Bishop

With reference to your minute of 15th October and telephone conversation on 14th October, the position is as follows:

The District Valuer was trying to make arrangements so that Mr Bishop would build new cattle sheds with the aid of a Ministry of Agriculture grant which he understood would amount to one-third of the cost of the sheds, subject to the design being approved by the Ministry. As the estimated cost was thought to be about £6,000 that would mean about £4,000 being found by this Department.

I understand from you that this was about the figure you and Finance had in mind and that you were influenced in agreeing to the proposal because there was a certain moral responsibility for pre-war promises and because the Ministry of Agriculture were going to give a grant.

The District Valuer has now discovered that the Ministry of Agriculture grant would not be one-third of the whole but one-third of the cost after deducting this Department's contribution! (Possibly we were a little optimistic to expect otherwise!) To add to the complication the builder's estimate for what was proposed appears to be higher than was anticipated. When the first builder's estimate, based on an architect's plan, was put to the District Valuer, the cost was of the order of £7,500 and he felt this was much too high. I agreed and verbally informed him that I considered £4,000 was the limit of the Department's contribution.

The District Valuer therefore proposed as a settlement that the Ministry of Transport be responsible for either two-thirds of the cost of the approved buildings or £4,000 whichever was the less.

Since it has been ascertained that the Ministry of Agriculture is working on a different basis from what was first understood, however, it is doubtful whether Mr Bishop is prepared to accept the Ministry's approved design and find the extra money. In view of this the District Valuer has decided to drop the proposal for constructing the new buildings and to deal with the matter purely on a compensation basis.

He estimates this compensation to be just about the proposed £4,000 figure, and so far as I can ascertain this will leave Mr Bishop to make his own arrangements for building cattle sheds on the eastern side of the By-Pass or alternatively to get rid of his cattle!

It is understood that Mr Bishop is likely to agree to the compensation and the only question then will be how quickly he can make arrangements for stopping his cows crossing the By-Pass. Presumably this will depend on how quickly he gets his money!

As a result of this the H.E.O. in the Division minuted an H.E.O. in the General Finance Division on October 28th:

In view of what we are now told about the basis of the Ministry of Agriculture contribution, we think that the arrangement to deal with the matter as proposed in the penultimate paragraph viz. under the normal compensation arrangements is quite satisfactory. Have you any comments please?

The reply on November 2nd was:

My only doubt about this was the possibility of the owner accepting the £4,000 but *not* building his cowsheds and allowing the cattle to continue to cross the road 4 times a day to the danger of the road users. However, you confirmed that this would not be possible as there would be no access from the farmlands to the Trunk Road.

In the circumstances, therefore, I agree to the District Valuer's proposal to offer £4,000 compensation, as a charge to the scheme.

This decision to treat the problem by way of compensation at £4,000 was given to the Divisional Road Engineer in a letter of November 11, 1956 as follows:

With reference to your minute of 21st May, it is confirmed that we had a figure of about £4,000 in mind as our contribution in connection with the building of the new cattle sheds. In view, however, of the basis, as now understood of the Ministry of Agriculture's grant, we agree with the decision to drop the proposal to construct the new buildings, and to deal with the matter on a compensation basis.

In April 1957 the builders started work on the new cowsheds and in May 1957 the sum of £4,000 plus legal costs was paid to Mr Bishop.

RE-HOUSING A PLOT-HOLDER

A New Home for Mrs Waters

When the Divisional Road Engineer's office forwarded on April 1, 1956 copies of the plot plans for each plot, he pointed out that it would be necessary to re-house the tenant of one of the plots. Permission to enter on the land was obtained by the District Valuer on May 7, 1956, but a minute of August 21, 1956 from the Divisional Road Engineer to Lands Branch explained that there were serious difficulties. This now follows:

X10 Trunk Road
Construction of Second Carriageway from Sheepwash to Roman
Monument
Plot No. 18

. . . We approached the Clerk to the Rural District Council of Roman Monument over the question of re-housing the tenant of this cottage at the end of March 1956 and at that time received an acknowledgement that the matter would be placed before the Council.

After a certain amount of informal communication with the Clerk to the Council an official reminder was sent on 11th August and the enclosed reply was received.

This is not very satisfactory from our point of view and it is for consideration what further steps should be taken. The tenant's husband farms a smallholding (fields rented from various owners) in the vicinity of Roman Monument which is why the Clerk's letter is couched in the terms it is.

We are faced with delaying the roundabout part of the scheme until the end of the contract in the hope that something will turn up, or omitting it from the contract and doing it separately at a later date, still relying on a house falling vacant close at hand.

As we are almost at the point of receiving the Contract Documents for final approval I do not want to have further delay caused by having to alter the Bill of Quantities and propose to make provisions for the roundabout to be the last item to be done.

Even so there is no guarantee that alternative accommodation for the tenant will be found in time.

I suggest that consideration might be given to offering the Rural District Council financial aid to construct a small dwelling on a suitable site nearby. I have said nothing of this to the Council of course but feel that such offer might enable them to take some positive action.

The letter referred to in the minute read as follows:

The Rural District of Roman Monument
15th August, 1956.

Dear Sir,

X10 Trunk Road
Improvement between
Sheepwash and Roman Monument

Your letter of the 11th instant to hand.

I regret that at present my Council are unable to offer Mrs Waters any accommodation, the reason being that unless a tenant gives notice there are no dwellings available.

At the moment, there are no houses in course of construction and the next programme is in a village too far from Roman Monument to be of any use to Mrs Waters.

If a house should become available in a village near Roman

45

Monument, I feel sure the Council will give your application sympathetic consideration.

Yours faithfully,

(Sd.) Clerk to the Council

The suggestion by the Divisional Road Engineer that the Ministry should offer the Rural District Council some financial aid towards the re-housing was taken up in the Lands Branch and the E.O.(A.S.) wrote to the Divisional Road Engineer on September 17th asking him to pursue it. Part of her letter is as follows:

I refer to your minute of 21 August.

Will you please approach the Roman Monument District Council and tell them that if they will help forward the Minister's scheme by building for Mrs Waters a suitable small dwelling house near her agricultural holdings, the Minister will pay the Council the capital equivalent of £22 1s 0d per annum for 60 years; i.e., as for a dwelling provided by a local housing authority for the purposes of re-development or slum clearance under Section 3(1) (a) (i) with Section 3(3) (a) of the Housing Subsidies Act, 1956. Will you please let me know the outcome.

You should in consultation throughout with the District Valuer secure that the Minister shall *not* become liable to the freeholders for a vacant-possession-value of plot 18, e.g. perhaps on issuing a Notice to Treat if and when necessary. This, of course, means that Mrs Waters' eventual re-housing should not take place until a day after the Minister completes the acquisition of plot 18 at its tenanted value *unless* the District Valuer has first obtained undertakings by the Vendors (i) not to re-let and (ii) not to claim vacant-possession-value, possibly in return for the Minister's paying them any net rent lost to them from Mrs Waters' having vacated plot 18 until completion of the acquisition by the Minister.

You will appreciate that it is not possible, at present, even to forecast an entry date for this plot, and if you do include the roundabout items in the present contract, you must bear in mind the possibility that plot 18 may not be available when required even if the roundabout is the last item to be done.

I have sent a copy of this minute to the Chief Valuer for the information of the District Valuer.

Shortly after, an unexpected solution to Mrs Waters' problem was found, as is shown by part of a report from the Dis-

46

trict Valuer to the Chief Valuer, which was sent in the usual
way to the Lands Branch:

29th September 1956.

X10 Trunk Road
Construction of Second Carriageway from Sheepwash Cross Roads
to Roman Monument
Plots Nos. 11, 11A, 15, 18 and 19 Mrs Waters

Permission to enter, as you know, has already been obtained
from the tenant, Mrs Waters, and this lady has provisionally
accepted the tenancy of one of the Ministry of Transport cottages[1]
which I understand will be available shortly. This will facilitate
obtaining early entry of Mrs Waters' cottage, etc. I will forward
all other details when available on this matter.

Final arrangements for re-housing Mrs Waters were pressed
forward, so that the contractors could get on with demolishing
her house to make way for the roundabout. The Divisional
Road Engineer reported to the Management Section of Lands
Branch on March 21, 1957:

The Clerk of the County Council has asked the County Architect to carry out the repairs to the living-room floor and install
the water supply.

He has forwarded a tenancy letter signed by Mrs Waters which
is enclosed herewith, and the date of commencement of tenancy,
as you will note, is 7th March.

The County Surveyor has written, meanwhile, about the
urgency of the entry on plot 18 of the Sheepwash Cross Roads
to Roman Monument scheme where Mrs Waters is at present.

I understand from the District Valuer that he holds a signed
permission to enter from Mrs Waters as well as from the Vendors
of the plot, and I am therefore advising the County Surveyor to
give Mrs Waters the usual formal notice that he proposes to effect
entry a few days after 7th March.

By March 17th, the Divisional Road Engineer was able to
report to Lands Branch that the County Surveyor had asked
Mrs Waters to give possession of her house not later than
March 28, 1957.

[1] The Ministry has power to acquire land and property required for road
improvements in advance of immediate need. In this case, the cottages had been
acquired in expectation that they would need to be demolished for road-widening,
but the need had not yet arisen.

Money Difficulties

From the Ministry's point of view the outcome was very satisfactory. Unfortunately from Mrs Waters' standpoint, this was not quite the end of the matter. On August 18, 1957, the surveyor acting on her behalf, wrote to the Secretary of the Ministry pointing out that she had moved to the Ministry of Transport cottage on March 7th and her claim against the Ministry had been agreed on May 10th, but she had not yet received the agreed compensation. As the delay was causing very considerable hardship to Mrs Waters he asked whether payment could be made at an early date.

The District Valuer's report was signed on May 20, 1957, and countersigned by the Chief Valuer on May 24, 1957. The amount of compensation was shown as £460. Ownership was complicated by being shared amongst three different freeholders, which raised some legal complications on which the Lands Branch had had to seek advice from the Treasury Solicitor's Conveyancing Division.

In view of the letter from Mrs Waters' surveyor, the H.E.O. (A.S.) sent a minute to the Treasury Solicitor's Conveyancing Division on September 9th, in the hope of reaching a means of paying the compensation quickly; after explaining the position he continued:

> . . . Letters were exchanged last summer between us about acquiring leasehold and tenant interests before the acquisition of the freehold interest had been completed, and in the last paragraph of your letter of 9th August 1957 you said you would look into any particular case where hardship was suffered under the present procedure. I shall, therefore, be grateful if you will consider whether in the case of Mrs Waters, tenant interest might be dealt with (by means of forms LB28; draft attached) before the freehold interests are completed.

On September 16th the Treasury Solicitor's office replied to the effect that although there was an element of risk in acquiring the tenant's interest before the freehold had been acquired, this was probably small, and agreed that payment of compensation should go forward.

Three days later another letter arrived from the surveyor pressing even more urgently for swift action and pointing out that it was over six months since Mrs Waters had been compelled to give up occupation of her cottage and the farming business which she carried on at Roman Monument.

In view of the Treasury Solicitor's advice Lands Branch were able to reply by sending a form of Receipt and Undertaking to be signed by the vendor and witnessed. This was signed on October 5, 1957, and on October 19, 1957, a payable order for £498 16s 2d being £460, the agreed amount of compensation, plus interest and surveyor's fees, was sent to the surveyor in settlement.[1]

ACQUISITION OF CROWN ESTATE LAND

Drafting a Submission for Valuation

The reference schedules (form T.R. 138) showed that a number of the plots of land were part of the Crown Estate. As two government bodies were concerned, a submission to the Chief Valuer's Department was agreed between them, whereby the District Valuer's assessment would be accepted by both. The process by which the terms of this joint submission were settled will now be described.

Negotiations were opened by a letter of March 15, 1956, from the E.O.(A.S.) to the Crown Estate Commissioners, which follows:

> I am directed by the Minister of Transport and Civil Aviation to state that, in connection with the improvement of the above-mentioned Trunk Road, the Minister is desirous of securing possession of land which it is understood is the property of your Department. I enclose a copy of a Drawing No. . . . which illustrates the land, comprising 100,236 square yards and which is situated in the parishes of Hinton, Puxton and Wentworth.
>
> In accordance with the customary practice the Minister proposes to refer the question of the valuation of the land to the Department of Inland Revenue, and I am to ask whether your

---

[1] It should be explained that since the date of this case, a scheme has been introduced permitting advance payments of compensation to be made in certain cases up to 90 per cent of the entitlement before completion of the conveyance; if this scheme had been in operation at the time of the Wentworth By-Pass, Mrs Waters would have qualified for an advance payment when entry was made on her property.

Department would wish to raise any objection to this course being followed.

Will you please return the plan with your reply.

This brought the following reply on April 16th, raising one of the several practical problems which needed settlement and agreement:

The Commissioners have been considering the plan which was enclosed with your letter of 15th March 1956 and the implications arising from the proposed improvement of the trunk road. This is the first indication which has been received in this office of the greater part of the scheme although, of course, the Wentworth By-Pass proposals were known.

It has not yet been possible to go into the matter in very great detail but a preliminary examination of the plan and assessment of its consequences have given rise to the following points.

Two farms, Puxton Lodge and Mote Lodge, are at present divided by the trunk road and have about 57 acres and 101 acres respectively on the West side of the road. It is at present possible, though difficult, to cross the road with tractors and other farm implements, as, owing to the nature of the road, the traffic, though dense, is relatively slow. When the road improvements have been carried out it will presumably be impossible to cross owing to the increased speed of the traffic and some other means will have to be found to link the Eastern and Western portions of the farms. A tunnel somewhere near the Manor Farm in Puxton is one suggestion and the Commissioners will be glad to be favoured with the Ministry's views on this matter . . .

. . . The Commissioners are agreeable to the valuation of the land to be sold to the Ministry being made by the Department of Inland Revenue and suggest that this be done, when the time comes, by means of a joint submission by this Office and your Department to the Chief Valuer setting out the terms of the sale.

Your plan is returned herewith but the Commissioners would like to be supplied with a copy of it as soon as you can arrange for this to be done.

On April 30th, the E.O. sent a copy of this letter to the Divisional Road Engineer for his comments, and also sent three copies to the office of the Chief Valuer at Somerset House. The Divisional Road Engineer replied by a minute dated May 7, 1956, the contents of which were sent to the

Crown Estate Commissioners by the Higher Executive Officer, in a letter of May 21st, which follows:

I refer to your letter dated 16th April 1956.

1. After consultation with the Divisional Road Engineer, Midshire Division, the following points arise:

(a) To build a tunnel or underpass near the Manor Lodge would cost approximately £10,000. It is considered that the volume of farm traffic across the trunk road would not justify this expenditure.

(b) With regard to the question of the slow speed of traffic, it is considered that this is a fast section of the road. There should not be an undue increase in speed when the second carriageway is constructed and any increased difficulty due to speed would probably be offset by the fact that the traffic on the trunk road would be unidirectional.

(c) The need for traffic to cross the trunk road has however been considered. At the junction with the Sheepwash Inn advantage is being taken of the wide central reservation to accommodate vehicles waiting to cross the second carriageway.

If you agree similar consideration could be given to make an appropriate opening at the reservation near Manor Lodge to accommodate farm vehicles wishing to cross the trunk road.

2. The Minister would be prepared to purchase both pieces of land adjoining plots 3 and 9 as set out in para 2 of your letter.

3. It is appreciated that the pieces of land marked 3 and 4 by you will be cut off from the farms of which they are part, but this is unavoidable. However, compensation for severance would, no doubt, be considered when the valuation of the land is being made by the District Valuer.

4. It is agreed that the valuation of the land to be acquired by the Minister be referred to the Chief Valuer by means of a joint submission and you will, no doubt, forward a draft for approval in due course.

A copy of the reference Plan is enclosed for your retention.

P.S. Possession of the land is desired on 15th July 1956. Will you agree to this please?

The reply from the Crown Estate Commissioners of June 2, 1956, based on discussion between their local agents and their tenants, raised further problems. For example, they agreed that a tunnel would be too expensive but thought that there should be two openings in the central reservation. The letter went on:

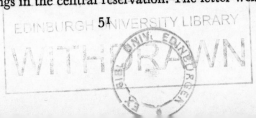

It is noted that possession of the land is desired on July, 15th 1956 and the Commissioners will be willing to grant this provided
> (a) the tenants are agreeable (two of them can insist on two months' notice if they wish) and
> (b) the terms of submission to the Chief Valuer have been agreed by then.

The Commissioners had arranged with a firm of timber merchants for the sale to them of certain trees in the strip of land which is now to be incorporated into the second carriageway. As it will not now be possible for the firm to remove the trees before July 15th the contract will have to be cancelled and the Commissioners assume that the Minister will agree to the price of the trees being included in the consideration money. Details of the firm and the price offered by them is being obtained for mention in the submission to the Chief Valuer.

On receipt of a favourable reply from you the joint submission will be prepared to embody the arrangement agreed and sent to you for your approval. In the meantime the Commissioners will notify the tenants of the urgency of the matter and obtain their provisional agreement to surrender the land by the date required.

One problem, that of the timber to be felled, was fortunately quickly solved; in a further letter the following day (June 3rd) the Crown Estate Commissioners said that it would after all be possible for the timber merchants to remove the trees by July 15th.

Gates, Hedges and Ditches: The Problems Resolved

The other problems proved less tractable and were in fact a prelude to a series of similar problems calling for agreement. As before, the E.O.(A.S.) sent a copy of the letter of June 2nd with a minute dated June 11th to the Divisional Road Engineer for his comments, and also on the same date sent three copies of it to the Chief Valuer's office asking that the Chief Valuer should obtain the tenant's agreement to entry on their land by July 15th, since the Crown Estate Commissioners' agreement was subject to agreement by their tenants. The Divisional Road Engineer replied on June 18th explaining how he was intending to meet the difficulties about farm crossings, and that provision had been made for the construction of the two crossings of the central reservation. On July 1st the H.E.O. passed on this information to the Crown Estate Commissioners, and ended his letter by saying that he would be glad to have a draft of the joint submission to the Valuation Office in due course.

On October 2, 1956, this draft joint submission was sent to the Lands Branch by the Crown Estate Commissioners, and again a copy was sent by the E.O.(A.S.) to the Divisional Road Engineer on October 13th for his comments. These came in a minute of October 20th. These comments mostly concerned such technical matters as the siting and type of drains and culverts, and after a good deal of further correspondence a meeting was held on the site on March 21, 1957, between representatives of the County Surveyor and of the Crown Estate Commissioners and the tenant of one of the plots. This led to most of the problems being resolved, but there were still some difficulties over gates and hedges which involved further correspondence.

On July 25, 1957, the Crown Estate Commissioners wrote to the H.E.O.(A.S.) saying that they were consulting their local agents about some of these points. In a further letter dated August 31st they raised further points, as a result of a submission of their agents; one of these concerned the provision of a gate into a field to avoid difficult and dangerous turns by farm vehicles.

The E.O. again sent copies of this correspondence to the Divisional Road Engineer, with a covering letter of September 26th asking for comments on the revised draft submission to the Valuation Office, and on October 15th he replied agreeing to some of the points which had been made by the Crown Estate Commissioners. Further correspondence followed on the subject of ditches and crossing places, of which the following is an example:

Extract from P. Phillips and Sons'
letter dated 11th January 1958
to Crown Estate Commissioners

We beg to report that we have had a letter from Mr Vale, Puxton Lodge Farm. He is very anxious about crossing. The contractors tell him that they have received instructions to form one opposite the main entrance to the farm and one opposite to the old carriage drive which serves the gate into OS . . . at the North-East corner of that field. This is all right as far as it goes, but it means that to get to OS . . . Mr Vale will have to go the whole length of the belt OS . . . down to the old carriage drive and then return up the length of OS . . . before he can get into the field, since the entrance to OS . . . is set in the North-East corner of this field.

A further crossing place between the North and South bound track is required opposite this gateway.

Yet another draft joint submission was now prepared in Lands Branch and this was sent by the E.O. to the Divisional Road Engineer on February 17, 1958, for comments. At the same time she asked that the crossing needed by Mr Vale could be provided. The Divisional Road Engineer replied by a minute of February 22, 1958, suggesting a few alterations to the draft submission and he agreed to provide a crossing for Mr Vale.

Again, on February 25, 1958, the draft submission further amended was sent to the Crown Estate Commissioners for agreement, and they replied on April 4, 1958, making several amendments. They also raised a new point, concerning sporting rights, leased to a Mr P. Barton Rensor. The Commissioners suggested that it would be convenient if the Chief Valuer could assess the abatement in rent due to Mr Barton Rensor in respect of the area to be sold.

The Commissioners' letter of April 4th was sent by the E.O. on April 24th to the Divisional Road Engineer as certain further points about crossing and ditches had been raised. The Divisional Road Engineer's reply in a minute of May 3, 1958, commented on the new points, and made the point that the contractor expected to be leaving the site shortly, and that any further work would have to be carried out by the County Council. He also said that '. . . Where possible, of course, I have not waited for the Crown Estate Commissioners' final agreement to accommodation works, and fortunately the bulk of the work has been done!'

On June 1, 1958, the E.O. wrote to the Commissioners passing on to them the Divisional Road Engineer's comments, contained in his minute of May 3rd, and this brought the following reply dated June 28, 1958:

I refer to your letter of the 1st June, on which I have consulted our local people. We act on their advice in technical matters, and I imagine that your Department also relies on local representatives in a similar way. I had assumed that solutions to such technical problems could be agreed between your local representatives and ours.

The amendments we made to the draft submission in this case were thought to embody local agreement on the points concerned. However, this does not seem to be so.

(There follow some technical points.)

... It does seem to be desirable that our local representative and yours should settle these technical questions locally before we engage in further correspondence on the draft submission. Perhaps they could get together and forward us both an agreed report on the size of the ditch, and diameter and position of the various pipes.

We could then modify the draft submission accordingly.

If you agree we will let our local people know and await the result.

In reply to this, the E.O. wrote on July 10th to say that the Divisional Road Engineer would get into touch with the Commissioner's local agents, and at the same time she sent a copy of this letter of June 28th from the Commissioners to the Divisional Road Engineer, asking him to get into touch with Messrs P. Phillips and Sons, the local agents, and to let her know what amendments to the draft submission were needed.

As regards the submission to the Chief Valuer, a good deal of further correspondence was necessary before a finally revised draft submission was agreed to by the Divisional Road Engineer on December 31, 1958, and by the Crown Estate Commissioners on February 4, 1959. On March 14, 1959, the E.O.(A.S.) was able to send two copies of the submission to the Superintending Valuer for the Midshire Region asking for a report of assessment of purchase price and compensation to be prepared by the District Valuer. Compensation was finally assessed at £1,740 plus surveyors' fees, but it was not until February 1961 that the conveyance was completed.

CONCLUSION

Some Administrative Problems

The selection of facts and of documents to be included in this narrative has been primarily governed by the consideration of the amount of space available and personal judgment of the degree of their importance. In certain places the narrative is abbreviated whereas in others documents are quoted in full. It has been necessary to decide at what stage to begin the story and where to end it. Furthermore, only certain parts have been chosen for inclusion, and others completely omitted.

All these decisions are to some extent arbitrary and subjective and may therefore reflect personal views. However, the factual material and the details of the method of presentation have not been adopted to prove or to disprove any particular thesis. No particular standpoint or administrative theory has been consciously adopted, but a certain emphasis and limitation has inevitably arisen from the method of preparation since the story as presented here is based entirely on the written evidence spread over a number of files in the Headquarters of the Ministry, and collated together.

The present account for this reason furnishes evidence only of what the events and problems look like to the Headquarters officials at all levels of the hierarchy concerned with the procedure. Even so, as the material has been collected and collated from a number of different files used by different Divisions and sections the picture presented here is probably larger than that with which the author of any particular letter or minute reproduced here would have been familiar.

Another type of emphasis and limitation arises from the fact that the narrative is based entirely and exclusively on written sources. Whilst these written documents were being located and assembled, a number of officials, including the authors of some of the documents reproduced here, expressed their views about their work, their problems and the system as a whole. Amongst these comments some contained points of criticism of certain aspects of the administrative system. A number of different attitudes were displayed, sometimes with considerable strength of feeling behind them. None of this is included in the story, partly because of limitations of time and space and primarily because the aim has been the illustration of the administrative machinery at work.

But the views, the feelings and attitudes of officials about the administrative machine of which they are a part have an important effect on the wording of their minutes and letters, and on the decisions they take. These factors therefore, both loyalties towards, and criticisms of, the administrative machinery are illuminating of the process of administration itself. However, to present this sort of picture is quite a different task from the one undertaken here.

This case study has been designed to show the administrative machine at work, and to provide as it were raw material showing the student of public administration how some of the present practices and customs in the British Civil Service work in detail. The student will form views about some of the problems involved in the working of the administrative system as illustrated here. There has been no attempt to indicate these in the course of the narrative, but it may be of use at this point to suggest a few possible lines of thought.

One problem is the balance between centralization and decentralization in this particular work. There is, in fact, some discussion within the Ministry about this. Parts of the story of the Wentworth By-Pass have special significance in this respect; for example, the account of the negotiations over the joint submission to the Valuation Office of Inland Revenue over the Crown Estate lands. To put forward full arguments on either side of the case would call for a separate essay. There are, however, arguments, not fully brought out here, in favour of a considerable degree of centralization, for example, in the central handling of the specialized legal work involved.

Another line of study is the advantages and disadvantages of the extensive use of stock letters and forms. An argument in their favour is that they permit of delegation of work to junior levels, and that this reduces the cost of the work because of economies in costs of salaries. As against this, there is the argument that work which has technical and specialist aspects has, as a result, to be undertaken by non-technical staff, and that their contribution therefore is limited to dealing with points which can be reduced to routine, and seeking technical advice on all other points. There is the further argument that if the work were decentralized more and put in the hands of technical staff, many of the stock forms and letters used for transmission of information from one section to another might become unnecessary.

But behind all these detailed and to some extent technical

points of administration lies the fundamental question which was touched on in the opening paragraphs of this case study; granted the importance of modernizing and improving our highway system, have we found the best and quickest means of putting this into effect? Here, inevitably, we come up against an old conflict, between the rights of the individual and the needs of the nation. A quicker system of land acquisition for example, might not be equally fair to the individuals whose land is being acquired. On the other hand, delay in modernizing our roads may have serious economic effects and may thus affect indirectly those most immediately concerned in the process of land acquisition. It would be foolish to pretend that this case study can solve that conflict, but what it can do is to provide some evidence on which to judge how far a detailed piece of administration can in practice achieve the right balance between speed and efficiency on the one hand and regard for the legitimate rights of the individual on the other. In this light one should judge the cases of Mrs Waters, and of Mr Bishop's cowsheds.

It is also worth remarking that a period of nearly two years elapsed from the date when the Treasury first gave approval to the Wentworth By-Pass scheme, among others, to the date when work on building the road began. To many this may seem a long time, but if so where in the whole process of planning and negotiation, and the considerable volume of correspondence and discussion to which they give rise, could savings be made?

These are some of the problems which a study of this typical piece of administrative work may raise. If the underlying thought left in the minds of many readers is the great complexity of the business of administration, this too may provoke reflection on the lessons to be learned from a study of administration in detail.

Appendix I

TRUNK ROADS ACT, 1946
Section 1, subsection (2)

The Minister shall keep under review the national system of routes for through traffic in Great Britain and if he is satisfied after taking into consideration the requirements of local and national planning, including the requirements of agriculture, that it is expedient for the purpose of extending, improving or reorganizing that system that any existing road, or any road proposed to be constructed by him, should become a trunk road, or that any trunk road should cease to be a trunk road, he may by order direct that a trunk road shall become, or as the case may be shall cease to be, a trunk road as from such date as may be specified on that behalf in the order.

Second Schedule

Procedure for Making Orders

Before making the order, the Minister shall publish in at least one local newspaper circulating in the area in which any road to which the order relates is situated and in the *London* or *Edinburgh Gazette*, as the case may be, a notice:

(a) stating the general effect of the order

(b) specifying a place in the said area where a copy of the draft order and of any relevant map or plan may be inspected by any person free of charge at all reasonable hours during a period of three months from the date of the publication of the notice; and

(c) stating that, within the said period, any person may by notice to the Minister object to the making of the order.

2. Not later than the date on which the said notice is published as aforesaid, the Minister shall serve a copy thereof (together with a copy of the draft order and of any relevant map or plan) on the council of every county, county borough, or metropolitan borough which any road to which the order relates is situated, and, in the case of a road situated in any other borough in an urban district, on the council of the borough or urban district.

4. If before the expiration of the said period of three months an objection is received by the Minister from any council on whom a notice is required to be served under this Schedule, or from any other person appearing to him to be affected by the order, and the objection is not withdrawn, the Minister shall cause a local inquiry to be held provided that except where the objection is made by any such council as aforesaid, the Minister may

dispense with such an inquiry if he is satisfied that in the special circumstances of the case the holding of such an inquiry is unnecessary.

5. After considering any objections to the order which are not withdrawn, and, where a local inquiry is held, the report of the person who held the inquiry, the Minister may make the order either without modification or subject to such modifications as he thinks fit.

N.B. These provisions now appear in Section 7 and the First Schedule of the Highways Act, 1959.

Appendix II

*X*10 *TRUNK ROAD (MIDSHIRE)*

Compulsory Purchase (No.   ) Order, 1957

The Minister of Transport and Civil Aviation hereinafter referred to as ('the Minister') in exercise of his powers under Section 13 of the Restriction of Ribbon Development Act 1935(a), as amended by or under any other enactment and as applied by section 4 of the Trunk Roads Act, 1936(b), Section 14 of the Special Roads Act, 1949(c), and section 1 of the Acquisition of Land (Authorisation Procedure) Act, 1946(d), and of all other powers him enabling in that behalf, hereby makes the following Order:

1. Subject to the provisions of this Order the Minister is hereby authorised to purchase compulsorily for the purposes of the improvement of that length of the X10 Trunk Road which extends from (here follows the precise description of the road and map reference); the construction of a new length of the X10 Trunk Road aforesaid from (here follows a precise description of the area to be covered by a new length of road) the lands which are described in the Schedule to this Order and are delineated and coloured pink on a plan marked 'The X10 Trunk Road (Midshire) Compulsory Purchase (No.   ) Order, 1957', and sealed with the Official Seal of the Minister and deposited at the Ministry of Transport and Civil Aviation, Berkeley Square House, London, W.1.

(a) 25 & 26 Geo.5.c.47   (c) 12, 13 and 14 Geo.6.c.32
(b) 1 Edw.8 & 1 Geo.6.c.5   (d) 9 & 10 Geo.6.c.49

2. Section 77 of the Railways Clauses Consolidation Act 1945(e) and sections 78 to 85 of that Act as originally enacted and not as amended for certain purposes by section 15 of the Mines (Working Facilities and Support) Act, 1923(f), are hereby incorporated with the enactments under which the foregoing purchase is authorised subject to the following modifications

references in the said sections to the company shall be construed as references to the Minister and references to the railway or works shall be construed as references to the land authorised to be purchased and any buildings or works constructed or to be constructed thereon.

3. For the purposes of the said section 78 of the Railways Clauses Consolidation Act, 1845, as incorporated in this Order, the prescribed distance in relation to any seam of minerals lying underland adjoining the works to be constructed upon the lands described in the Schedule to this Order shall be such a lateral distance from the said works on every side thereof as is equal at every point along the said works to one half of the depth of the seam below the natural surface of the ground at that point or forty yards whichever is the greater.

4. The Interpretation Act, 1889(g), shall apply to the interpretation of this Order as it applied to the interpretation of an Act of Parliament.

5. This Order may be cited as 'The X10 Trunk Road (Midshire) Compulsory Purchase No.   Order 1957.'

Given under the Official Seal of the Minister of Transport and Civil Aviation this tenth day of October, 1956.

P. G. R. TOWNSEND
An Assistant Secretary of the
Ministry of Transport and Civil Aviation

(e) 8 & 9 Vict.c.20.   (f) 13 & 14 Geo.5.c.20.

II

New Standards of Accommodation for the Crews of Merchant Ships

THE PREPARATION OF THE MERCHANT SHIPPING (CREW ACCOMMODATION) REGULATIONS, 1953

CONTENTS

The Ministry of Transport and Crew Accommodation

This case study is concerned with the work of the Ministry of Transport in preparing detailed Regulations governing the conditions of accommodation for crews of British merchant ships. As will be seen, matters affecting merchant seamen are increasingly the subject of international discussion and agreement, and this study is therefore very much concerned with international obligations on the one hand, and the particular needs of the British Shipping industry on the other. How the Ministry of Transport attempts to reconcile the different interests involved may therefore be regarded as one of the main themes of the study. It should however be remarked at the outset that a particular feature of the case is the fact that for the most part the work is handled by senior officers of the Ministry. We are here concerned with the work particularly of Principals and to some extent of Assistant Secretaries, in the Administrative Class, and with corresponding officers in the Professional Classes, particularly the Principal Surveyor for Tonnage. Thus the work of the Ministry of Transport is viewed from a rather different angle from that of *The Wentworth By-Pass* case. There, the routine work of land acquisition procedure was the main concern, whereas here it is much more the questions of policy which arise, not on the whole questions of major policy, but nevertheless of very great importance to the shipowners, shipbuilders and officers and men of the Merchant Navy who are most immediately and directly affected by them. Before coming to the main narrative, it may be useful to indicate briefly how questions of crew accommodation fit into the Ministry's wider concerns.

If we regard the Ministry of Transport as being concerned with two major separate subjects, Inland Transport and Shipping, and Marine matters as only one of several concerns of the part of the Ministry dealing with Shipping, we begin to get some idea of how crew accommodation occupies a small but significant place in the total activity of the Ministry. It is useful, however, to bear this in mind when reflecting on the narrative of this case, partly because in isolating the case in this manner it is easy to lose sight of the fact that much else was going on at the same time and claiming the attention of many of the people concerned in the narrative. The position may be summarized as follows: of three Under Secretaries in the Ministry concerned with shipping matters, one, known as the Under Secretary (Marine), has charge of three divisions, including the Crews Division; each of these divisions is in the charge of an Assistant Secretary. Crew accommodation is one of a number of subjects which are the concern of the Assistant Secretary of the Crews Division.

It may be as well to state here that throughout the case study the officers referred to as the 'Under Secretary', the 'Assistant Secretary' and the 'Principal' without any other qualification are, respectively, the Under Secretary in charge of the Marine Group of Divisions, the Assistant Secretary in charge of the Marine Crews Division and the Principal in that Division specifically concerned with matters affecting the accommodation of crews.

So far only the administrative structure of the Ministry concerned with the accommodation of crews has been considered. But two other people, or perhaps one should say, sets of people in government departments play an important part in the case. One is the Treasury Solicitor's Department which, as was seen in *The Wentworth By-Pass* case, undertakes the legal work needed by the Ministry; in this case the Department will be seen putting the legal stamp on hard-won agreements, to make the final product an acceptable legal instrument carrying the force of law.

But even more important in the detailed narrative is the part played by the Ministry's own professional staff, and in particular, the marine surveyors. Drafting and getting agreement on Regulations is not something which can be done in a vacuum. The Regulations are going to have a practical effect, in this case on the design of ships and on the lives of the men who serve in them. Moreover, somebody has to see that these practical effects do in fact take place, that is, that the Regulations are followed. This is the task of the Ministry's Marine Surveyors who are for the most part stationed at the ports, and have powers of inspection of ships. Many of the duties of the Surveyors are concerned with inspecting the safety arrangements of ships, since it is a major concern of central government, in shipping matters, to ensure that reasonable standards of safety are maintained. In part, the question of crew accommodation is also concerned with safety, although, as will be clear from the narrative, it goes very much wider than that.

The survey service is organized administratively in nine districts each under the charge of a Principal Officer,[1] but there is also a Headquarters Staff and these naturally appear more prominently in the narrative since this case deals more with the advance planning than with the day-to-day administration at the ports. Closely concerned with the negotiations is the Principal Surveyor for Tonnage. His title reflects another part of the Surveyor's work, the measurement of ships for tonnage. The details of this work do not concern this case but there is an important distinction between gross and net tonnage to be noted. In assessing net tonnage a deduction is made from the gross tonnage of those parts of the ship which do not produce revenue, foremost among these being the parts used for the accommodation of the crew. It is this aspect of survey work for which the Principal Surveyor for Tonnage (or 'P.S.T.' as he will henceforth be called for brevity) is the Ministry's chief expert; and it is for this reason that the P.S.T. rather than any of the other Headquarters survey staff takes the chief part in discussions. The Chief Ship Surveyor (or 'C.S.S.') does however appear from time to time since he is the Ministry's chief naval architect, and crew accommodation is basically concerned with ship construction.

The National Maritime Board

A major part of this case is concerned with the detailed negotiations undertaken by the Ministry of Transport with the outside interests most directly concerned, that is, the shipowners and the merchant seamen, to secure agreement on the Regulations. For the most part, these negotiations were conducted

---

[1] Not to be confused with an (Administrative) Principal; the Principal Officer is of equivalent rank to the Principal Surveyor for Tonnage (see below) and in terms of salary ranks somewhat below an Assistant Secretary but above a Principal.

with the National Maritime Board (generally referred to here as the 'N.M.B.'), a body with representatives from both sides of the shipping industry which is able to speak and negotiate with authority on matters directly affecting the industry.

The N.M.B. is not a statutory body but was set up by the industry in 1920[1] at a time when the need was felt for closer co-operation between employers and employed in negotiating on matters of mutual concern, especially those relating to wages and conditions of service. The Board has 144 members, 72 representing employers and 72 representing employees. On the employers' side, three-quarters of the members are appointed by the Shipping Federation Limited, a body formed in 1890 as an association of shipowners. A separate organization, the Employers' Association of the Port of Liverpool, also appoints members to the Board, as does the Marine Wireless Employers' Negotiations Committee, as the members of both these bodies employ seafarers in addition to the members of the Shipping Federation. Finally, by invitation of the employers' representatives, there are two co-opted members of the Board representing the Railways Board and the Admiralty.

On the employees' side, the following bodies are represented:

Elected Sea-going Masters
The Mercantile Marine Service Association
The Merchant Navy and Airline Officers' Association[2]
The Amalgamated Engineering Union
The Radio Officers' Union
The National Union of Seamen
The Shipconstructors' & Shipwrights' Association

Of these, the National Union of Seamen represents the great bulk of the ratings.

As might be expected, a great deal of the work is done not in full meetings of the Board, but either through specialized panels concerned with particular groups, such as engineer officers or sailors and firemen, or through functional committees set up to deal with particular issues. In the present case, a Crew Accommodation Committee was set up by the Board to

---

[1] A body with the same name had been set up on Government initiative during the 1914–18 war, but as a temporary measure to deal with wartime problems.

[2] Formed by an amalgamation of the Navigators' and Engineer Officers' Union and the Marine Engineers' Association.

undertake detailed consideration of the Regulations but the Small Ships and Day Ships Committee also took part in some of the negotiations. Such committees, like the Board itself, have representatives drawn from both sides of the industry, although not necessarily in equal proportions. Decisions taken by the Board are binding on the members of the various constituent bodies.

Although much of the formal negotiations in the present case took place between the Ministry of Transport and the Crew Accommodation Committee of the N.M.B., there was also a good deal of informal and preliminary discussion on particular points. Examples will be found in the narrative of this case of discussions taking place with the shipowners' side of the Crew Accommodation Committee alone or even with individual owners. The general principle was that the Ministry were prepared to discuss individual points with either side in this way, but it was understood that final agreement could only be reached after discussion with both sides. Discussions of this kind were in turn quite separate from the internal discussions which were going on all the time within the Ministry, within the N.M.B., and within each of the two sides of the N.M.B.

Crew Accommodation until 1945

This case is concerned mostly with events since 1945, but the position before that date may be briefly summarized.

The State was drawn into the field of safety and well-being of seafarers in the nineteenth century, much as it was drawn into other similar fields, by a gradual realization of the inadequacies and defects of the existing system, one result of which was a decline (or feared decline) in British commercial supremacy.[1] The story of the Plimsoll Line is perhaps the most familiar of the many efforts which were made to deal with the scandal of loss of life at sea, efforts which culminated in the Merchant Shipping Act of 1894, the foundation of much of present practice and not least of the attempt to regulate standards of accommodation for crews of merchant ships.

Indeed, until 1954, Section 210 (and the Sixth Schedule) of

[1] For a brief account see Sir Gilmour Jenkins, *The Ministry of Transport and Civil Aviation*, George Allen & Unwin, 1959, pp. 27–33.

the 1894 Act remained the only legislative provision on the subject.[1] Only the amount of space per man was specifically laid down, and for the rest the provisions were vague. The penalty for not complying was a fine on the owner of £20 for each offence; but perhaps a more effective sanction was that the Board of Trade's surveyors[2] could refuse to deduct crew spaces from gross tonnage, the effect being to increase the dues paid by the owners (e.g. for the use of docks), which were based on net tonnage.

In addition to the legislation, the Board issued detailed 'Instructions to Surveyors', laying down more precise standards of what should be provided by way of crew accommodation. These were revised in 1937 in a much more detailed form than before, to conform with the generally accepted and improved standards of the day.

These new Instructions thus represented agreed standards, and reflected the existing practice of the more enlightened owners. They did not have the force of law, but depended for their success on the persistence and persuasion of the Surveyors and the good will of the shipbuilders and shipowners. Their intention was to lay down minimum standards on such points as the minimum height of accommodation, protection from effluvium, heat and moisture, separate accommodation for different ratings, provision of hospitals and lighting and ventilation standards.

This was the position until after the 1939–45 war, when international interest in these questions provided the first main stimulus to further action.

The Copenhagen Conference of 1945

Ever since the International Labour Organization (I.L.O. for short) was set up as part of the machinery of international conciliation at the end of the First World War, it has been the principal body concerned with international discussion of problems of labour relations, including those of the shipping industry. But, no doubt because of the peculiar conditions of

---

[1] Apart from an amendment made by the Merchant Shipping Act, 1906.
[2] The Mercantile Marine Department of the Board of Trade was the responsible government department for this legislation until 1939.

life at sea, seamen's problems have always been considered in separate maritime conferences.[1] Not only Government representatives, but representatives of shipowners and seafarers meet at these conferences, and the results of their discussions emerge as either Conventions, Recommendations or Resolutions. The difference between these three is primarily a matter of the degree of force which they carry; we shall be chiefly concerned with Conventions, which are the most binding form of agreement.

After the Second World War there was a general movement to improve the standards of health and welfare of workers. So far as standards of accommodation for crews on board ship were concerned, the first moves were made by the I.L.O. in 1945. On the basis of a survey of existing practice in a number of countries (including Great Britain) and of the views put forward by an international meeting of seafarers' representatives in 1944, an I.L.O. Maritime Preparatory Technical Conference meeting at Copenhagen in that year prepared a draft Convention on the subject of crew accommodation. This draft was put forward for consideration at a full Maritime Conference held in Seattle, U.S.A. in 1946. The I.L.O. added the following comment on the draft:

The question is a new one from an international point of view, and only a limited amount of guidance can be obtained from existing national regulations. There are, however, a number of arguments in favour of reaching international agreement on minimum standards as early as possible. It was generally agreed at Copenhagen that the merchant navies of the United Nations had made a magnificent contribution to the war effort, and that it would be only fitting, in return, to do everything possible to improve the living and working conditions of merchant seamen which had, in the past, frequently lagged behind those of their fellow-workers in shore industries. It was further recognized that the ship is not merely the seafarer's place of employment; it is his home for a very large part of his life. If the best type of man is to be attracted to service at sea, he must be offered the best possible conditions of accommodation compatible with technical efficiency and profitable operation.

[1] For this reason the Ministry of Transport and not the Ministry of Labour provide the U.K. Government delegations to these conferences.

They also pointed out that there was some urgency in the matter since a great many ships had been sunk during the war and were likely to be replaced in the near future.

The Seattle Conference of 1946

The United Kingdom Government agreed generally with the intentions behind the conference, particularly as there was a realization that existing legislation needed to be brought up to date. As a first stage, a meeting was held in the Ministry of Transport on April 15, 1946, attended by the Deputy Secretary (Shipping), the Assistant Secretary and the P.S.T. to consider the proposals in the draft Convention. This was a preliminary to discussions with the N.M.B. with the object of trying to reach as close an agreement as possible before the Seattle meeting.

Following the meeting on April 15th, a number of suggested U.K. amendments to the I.L.O. proposals were drafted and sent to the N.M.B. for circulation to the members of their Crew Accommodation Committee. At the end of April 1946, a meeting was held at the Ministry between representatives of the Ministry, i.e. the Under Secretary, the Assistant Secretary, and the P.S.T., and the National Maritime Board Committee on Crew Accommodation, consisting of 18 shipowners' representatives, and 8 representatives of seafarers' unions.

The meeting considered the Ministry's amendments which had been circulated in advance. On most points agreement was reached, but on a number of outstanding points it was decided to try to reach agreement either before the conference or at the conference itself. It was agreed that at Seattle the three sections[1] should keep in touch with one another, and one of the Ministry contingent said that it would be desirable for the British delegation to adhere to the lines so far agreed, if they were to secure acceptance of the British amendments at the Seattle Conference.

Representation at the Conference was on a tripartite basis, each country being invited to send delegations representing the Government, the employers and the workers, and the various committees which were constituted to carry out the detailed work of the Conference were also based on this division

[1] i.e. Ministry, Shipowners and Unions.

into three groups. Since the three groups were not necessarily equal in numbers the voting arrangements were usually adjusted to give equal weight to each group. Thus the Crew Accommodation Committee at Seattle consisted of 18 Government members,[1] 12 members representing employers and 12 representing workers. Each Government vote counted as two, and each employer's and worker's vote as three.

In spite of the amicable start which the British discussions had made, difficulties soon arose at the Conference. For example the twelve shipowners' representatives had, after a short while, declared that they were not prepared to discuss the text of the draft until the position in regard to existing ships had been cleared. This led to delay while they prepared a memorandum presenting their point of view together with a revised text, but it was only with the greatest difficulty that a version was agreed which was acceptable to everyone. But there were also fundamental differences of approach. The American delegation, for example, were anxious to secure a Convention which stated quite specifically in every case what must and must not be applied by the competent authority to a ship. It is not surprising that a report from the U.K. Government delegate (the Assistant Secretary) described the situation in these words: 'We have had a very stormy time over absolutely everything here', but the final agreement was reasonably satisfactory from the point of view of the U.K. Government.

The White Paper of 1947

To give effect to the Convention adopted at Seattle (known as Convention No. 75), the U.K. Government would have to enact laws or regulations, and amend existing legislation as appropriate. The Ministry of Transport recognized that the negotiating machinery of the shipping industry was preoccupied with urgent questions arising from the termination of the war-time organization of the industry and, taking this into account, aimed to reach decisions about the ratification of the Conventions and other matters in time for a White Paper to be

[1] One each from Belgium, Canada, Chile, China, Denmark, France, India, Italy, the Netherlands, Norway, Portugal, New Zealand, Mexico, Sweden, Turkey, the United Kingdom, the United States and Venezuela.

laid before Parliament by December 28, 1947, i.e. eighteen months after the closing of the I.L.O. Session at which Convention No. 75 was drawn up. Eighteen months is the maximum period under the I.L.O. constitution within which Conventions must be brought by members before a competent authority within their country to decide whether the Convention is to be ratified or what other action is to be taken upon it.

As a first step informal consultations with the N.M.B. were begun on the basis of outline notes prepared by the Ministry on the various questions. The note on Convention No. 75, relating to crew accommodation, dated May 8, 1947, was prepared by the Assistant Secretary. After pointing out that the Convention applied generally to all seagoing mechanically-propelled vessels of 500 gross tons and over, but was also to be applied where reasonable and practicable to new vessels between 200 and 500 gross tons, he made the following suggestion for the new legislation which would be needed:

> The most satisfactory course would probably be to include power to prescribe standards of crew space by regulation in a Bill conferring enabling powers etc. in respect of all Seattle Conventions which can be ratified and to which effect cannot be given by collective agreements. As soon as the Regulations were made the Convention could be ratified, and the powers conferred could be exercised to prescribe higher standards at a later date, as they become necessary.

During discussions with the National Maritime Board on this Convention, some difficulties were discovered in the precise application of all the details. It was therefore decided that the Convention should not be ratified as it stood. A White Paper was presented to Parliament by the Minister of Labour and National Service in November, 1947, stating the action proposed by the Government as a result of the various Conventions and Recommendations adopted at Seattle. In the case of Convention No. 75 on Crew Accommodation, the White Paper said the following:

> Legislation is proposed to amend certain provisions of the Merchant Shipping Acts relating to crew accommodation and to enable regulations to be made on this subject.

Both sides of the industry have asked that, if this Convention is ratified, a reservation should be made in regard to the requirement contained in Article 10 (9) that not more than four deck and engine-room ratings may be accommodated in a single room. They desire that this should be altered to permit of as many as ten being so accommodated, as is provided for catering ratings in Article 10 (10). His Majesty's Government agree that this is desirable in the larger types of passenger ships in the interests of the men concerned, many of whom would otherwise be deprived of natural ventilation and lighting. They therefore propose to inform the International Labour Office that they are unable to ratify the Convention so long as this provision remains, but it is their intention, in consultation with the industry, to adopt regulations covering all other matters dealt with in the Convention.[1]

The Merchant Shipping Act of 1948

The proposal in the White Paper did not give rise to any discussion in Parliament and a Merchant Shipping Bill on the lines indicated and including provisions resulting from other Conventions affecting merchant shipping which the Government was prepared to ratify as they stood, was drafted. During the course of drafting, a number of difficulties arose in giving legal effect to the practical intentions of the Seattle Convention. In particular, there was a problem over the application of the terms of the Convention to existing ships.

The Seattle Convention provided that existing ships, that is, those whose keels were laid before the date of the Convention becoming operative for the territory where the ship was registered, would be held to comply with the provisions of the Convention on certain conditions. These were that, if the ship was below the standard set by the Convention, alterations might be required to bring it into conformity, in so far as the competent authority[2] 'after consultation with the organizations of shipowners and/or the shipowners and with *bona fide* trades unions of seafarers, deems possible having regard to the practical problems involved, when (a) the ship is re-registered; (b) substantial structural alterations or major repairs are made to the vessel as a result of long-range plans and not as a result of

---

[1] Cmd. 7273, p. 5.   [2] i.e. in this country, the Minister of Transport.

accident or emergency'. A similar provision was included to cover ships in process of building.

This provision allowing discretion to the competent authority had been adopted by vote at the Seattle Conference following a certain amount of discussion and argument. The workers' representatives had pressed for the application of the minimum standards of crew accommodation to existing as well as new ships, but the employers had argued that it would be technically impossible or economically unsound to alter all existing ships to bring them up to the new standards. The difficulty which arose on the drafting of the 1948 Bill was to devise a satisfactory procedure which would give effect to the intention behind this provision, and this point was discussed by the Ministry with both sides of the industry in the N.M.B.

Another difficulty was the application of this provision to any foreign, Colonial or Dominion ship at the time when she came on to the U.K. registry. Although it would be easy to do this for those ships whose keels were laid before the date on which the Convention became operative, it would be impossible for the 'existing ship' provision to be applied to a foreign, Dominion or Colonial ship built after that date and then coming on to the U.K. registry, and it would have to comply with the full extent of the Convention requirements. This would mean that a British shipowner who bought such a ship from a country which had not adopted the Convention would have to alter her to comply with the full range of Convention standards. Such a ship (e.g. an American one) might have a very high standard of accommodation, but because she differed from the Convention pattern, she might have to be completely reconstructed. It was therefore desirable that the new Bill should not be framed in such a way as to make the transfer to the U.K. registry of such a ship a difficult or impossible procedure.

Because of difficulties of this kind, the drafting of the Bill took some time, but on February 4, 1948, the Assistant Secretary was able to report that, as a result of the discussions which had been held with both shipowners and unions following the Seattle Conference, the Bill was likely to go forward as a non-controversial measure which was acceptable to the Ministry and to both sides of the industry.

In the same month the Bill was presented to Parliament, and

76

went through all the usual stages unchanged except for one minor amendment, receiving the Royal Assent on July 13, 1948. It gave the Minister of Transport powers, 'after consultation with such organization or organizations as appear to him to be representative both of owners of British ships and of seamen employed therein, (to) make regulations with respect to the crew accommodation to be provided in ships of any class specified in the regulations'.

For ships already built, or in process of construction, the Act provided that an application should be made by the owner of the ship to the Minister and if, after consultation with the owner or an organization representing owners and an organization representing British seamen, the Minister considered that such steps as were 'reasonable and practicable' had been taken for securing compliance with the Regulations, the ship could be certified accordingly. Similarly, application to the Minister could be made in respect of any ship not on the United Kingdom register before the date when the regulations came into force, and subsequently registered in the United Kingdom. The Regulations were to apply in full to ships of which the keels were laid after the date of their coming into force, but not to fishing boats, ships belonging to the three general lighthouse authorities, and pleasure yachts.

Now that the Merchant Shipping Act had been passed, the way seemed clear for the final framing of the Regulations, in consultation with both sides of the industry, so that they could be embodied in a Statutory Instrument. But first there was one outstanding problem to be settled.

Geneva Conference, 1949: Seattle Convention Modified

It has been pointed out that the shipping industry, both employers' and workers' sides, had certain reservations about the Seattle Convention, although they were in agreement with the great majority of its provisions. The United Kingdom was not alone in having certain doubts. Other Governments also wished to introduce amendments to the Convention before they would be willing to ratify it. It was therefore decided that there should be discussions on the revision of some of the Seattle Conventions at the I.L.O. meeting at Geneva in 1949.

In addition to the modification mentioned in the White Paper, the United Kingdom proposed others, in particular provision for variations in design from the exact specifications of the Convention, if the Ministry after consultation with the organizations of shipowners and seafarers were satisfied that the variations to be made would 'provide corresponding advantages as a result of which the overall conditions are not less favourable than the actual compliance with the Convention'. Particulars of all such cases would be sent by the Ministry to the International Labour Office, who would notify all members of the International Labour Organization. The intention of this amendment was to allow experiments in design, rather than have a rigid code which might, in practice, instead of being a minimum standard come to be treated as a final standard and a bar to further progress in design.

The Under Secretary and the Assistant Secretary attended the 32nd Session of the International Labour Conference at Geneva in June 1949. The General Conferences did not usually deal with maritime matters, which were usually considered by the special Maritime Conferences, but on this occasion it was thought that it would be simpler to deal with certain specified points arising from the Seattle Conventions in this way.

The British Government delegates were a Deputy Secretary and an Under Secretary from the Ministry of Labour and National Service. The Under Secretary and Assistant Secretary from the Ministry of Transport were technically advisers on maritime matters, but in practice handled all maritime matters both in committee and in the plenary Conference, until the record vote was taken on the last day. The maritime matters were at once remitted to a special Sub-Committee on the Revision of Maritime Conventions, with representatives of Governments, employers and workers. This Committee considered in turn the specific suggestions for revision of the Seattle Conventions, which had been circulated in advance by the International Labour Office, including those for the Convention on Crew Accommodation (No. 75).

The U.S.A. Government member had instructions to oppose all amendments to this Convention, on the grounds that the U.S.A. was anxious that nothing should be done to weaken the

Convention. In the event, all the suggested amendments were in fact carried by majority vote. The United Kingdom amendment which would allow building of experimental ships, was easily carried. So also was the amendment permitting up to ten ratings of any department to sleep in one sleeping-room, provided that there was prior consultation with the organizations of shipowners and seafarers' unions.

As a result of the discussions and acceptance of amendments at Geneva, a new Convention was drawn up, No. 92. So far as the U.K. Government were concerned this removed the obstacle to ratification of Convention No. 75, once the necessary legislation had been agreed.

The way was now clear for the Regulations to be drafted, and indeed preliminary work had already begun while the 1948 legislation was going through Parliament. The main part of this case is concerned with how the Regulations reached their final form and this is described in detail below. But in order not to hold up the narrative it may be convenient to mention here a further piece of legislation which was enacted during the course of the negotiations.

A Legal Difficulty: The Merchant Shipping Act, 1952

The procedure adopted was first to discuss and agree a draft of the Regulations in non-legal language. When this had been done, the Treasury Solicitor[1] was in a position to prepare the legal version embodied in a Statutory Instrument. The reason for this procedure, which is quite commonly adopted, is to make discussion of what are often detailed and technical matters easier before the Regulations are put into formal and precise legal language.

By the end of March 1951 the first stage had been completed, but before the Treasury Solicitor could set to work on the Regulations, a major legal difficulty had to be overcome. The Ministry wished to be in a position to approve accommodation of as good a standard as that laid down in the Regulations, even though it did not precisely conform to the Regulations. As this

---

[1] Here and elsewhere in this case, 'Treasury Solicitor' refers to the Ministry of Transport Branch of the Treasury Solicitor's Department.

was not possible under existing powers, fresh legislation was prepared to meet the point.

The Bill was successfully steered through the House and enacted on March 13, 1952. There was some opposition and the rather caustic comments of the *Journal of Commerce* for December 5, 1951, throw light on some of the arguments for and against the Bill:

> Although Cmdr H. Pursey, Socialist Member for East Hull was no doubt exaggerating somewhat when he remarked that two of his Party colleagues in the House, Sir Richard Acland and Mr James Johnson 'don't know the sharp end from the blunt end of a ship' they nevertheless were ill-advised, to put it mildly, to move the rejection of a Merchant Shipping Bill which all sections of the shipping industry and the vast majority of members of Parliament, approve. The purpose of the Bill is, as the Minister of Transport pointed out, to enable him to make exemptions from requirements as to crew accommodation proposed in the Merchant Shipping Acts of 1948 and 1950.[1]
>
> There is no question at all of the Bill's nature. It will not, contrary to what Sir Richard Acland and Mr Johnson considered, 'relieve merchant shipping companies of costs in connection with crews, at a time when increases in freight charges should have left them ample resources to meet this expenditure'. What it will do is to allow owners who so wish to depart from orthodox practices, as far as accommodation is concerned, always provided that they at least conform to minimum standards as required by the Acts, and the Minister to grant exemption in cases where it would be impossible for a particular ship fully to comply with the provisions of the Acts. . . . Only those unfamiliar with the aims and policies of the shipping industry and the Ministry of Transport would suggest that to give the Minister power to exempt certain ships from hard-and-fast accommodation rules would be a retrograde step; only those ignorant of the character of British owners and the strength of seafarers' representative organizations would believe that the former wish to reduce the amount of money they spend on providing quarters for crews, or that the latter would approve granting to the Minister powers of exemption if they thought that lower accommodation standards might result.

As will be shown when the discussions with the industry are

[1] The 1950 Act concerned fishing vessels.

described, both sides of the industry were willing for the power of exemption to be given to the Minister, in order to ensure that the Regulations should apply to as many types of ship as possible. If there had been no provision for exemption, either the Regulations would not have touched certain types of ship at all, or the general standard would have had to be so lowered that all types of ship could come within them. This legislation became the Merchant Shipping Act of 1952.

DRAFTING THE REGULATIONS

Discussing the First Draft: Meeting with N.M.B.

The Regulations, as finally agreed by the Ministry, the shipowners' and the seafarers' representatives, were published as Statutory Instrument No. 1036 of 1953. These forty pages give precise details of the requirements on everything from the height of accommodation to the provision of medical cabinets. The thoroughness of the standards which they impose strike the reader at once; nothing seems to be left to chance, as may be judged from the following extract relating to the size of beds (Regulation 17(9)):

(a) Subject to the provisions of sub-paragraph (6) of this paragraph the size of the beds provided for the crew shall be at least 6 feet 3 inches by 2 feet 3 inches, the measurements being taken inside the lee-boards or lee-rails, if any, and at right angles to each other.
(b) The size of the beds provided in a ship of 3,000 tons or over for the Chief Officer and for the Chief and Second Engineers shall be at least 6 feet 3 inches by 2 feet 9 inches in a passenger steamer and at least 6 feet 3 inches by 3 feet 6 inches in any other ship, the measurements in each case being taken inside the lee-boards or lee-rails, if any, and at right angles to each other.

Each of the provisions of these Regulations was considered, by all three parties that is, shipowners, unions and Ministry, discussed fully among them, and if there was disagreement, rediscussed and in many cases amended. This process will now be described, and examples will be given of some of the problems both of substance and of drafting which arose during this preparatory stage.

F

Both the Seattle Convention No. 75, and the Geneva Convention No. 92 laid down that the 'competent authority' must consult the organizations of shipowners and/or the shipowners and also the recognized *bona fide* trade unions of seafarers in regard to the framing of Regulations, and to collaborate so far as practicable with such parties in the administration thereof (Article 3). So far as the United Kingdom was concerned the work of examining and agreeing on the form of the Crew Accommodation Regulations was undertaken by the Ministry together with the National Maritime Board mostly through the latter's Crew Accommodation Committee.

By January, 1950, a draft of new Regulations designed to give effect to the provisions of the Seattle and Geneva Conventions had been prepared in the Ministry by the Assistant Secretary who had attended the two International Labour Office meetings at Seattle and Geneva, the Principal and the P.S.T. This draft was sent to the N.M.B., with a covering letter from the Assistant Secretary, dated January 5, 1950.

To quote from part of this letter:

> The National Maritime Board will be aware that the Minister has under consideration the formulation of Crew Accommodation Regulations under powers conferred on him by Section 1 of the Merchant Shipping Act, 1948.
>
> . . . These Regulations will give effect to the standards now current and of general adoption in the ships built in recent years in the United Kingdom, and also to the provisions of the Convention on Crew Accommodation (revised) No. 92 which was adopted at the 32nd International Labour Conference at Geneva in 1949.
>
> In accordance with the provisions of Section 11 of the Merchant Shipping Act, 1948, the Regulations will take the form of a Statutory Instrument. It is proposed, however, to supplement them by instructions to Surveyors designed to give guidance on matters of detail which cannot suitably be included in the Regulations themselves.

The letter went on to say that the draft had not been prepared in legal language, as it was thought it would be better for it to be discussed first on the basis of a draft in everyday language, and then, after agreement for it to be drafted as a legal instrument. The Board were asked to examine the draft, and send their comments to the Ministry after which discussions would be arranged. The instructions to Surveyors were to be sent to the Board later as they were not then ready.

At the same time, the draft was sent on January 5, 1950, by the Assistant Secretary to each of the Principal Officers at the ports, and to officers in other parts of the Ministry whose work might be affected by the introduction of the Regulations (e.g. the Chief Ship Surveyor).

When sending the draft Regulations to the Principal Officers, the Assistant Secretary asked for any comments on the content of the proposals. This was because it would ultimately be the province of the Ship Surveyors, who were members of their staffs, to administer the Regulations when finally settled, and clearly their comments were likely to be of practical value in the framing of the Regulations. A number of comments were received from the Principal Officers and these were considered by an internal meeting at the Ministry Headquarters of the Assistant Secretary, the Principal and the P.S.T. This meeting took place on February 16, 1950.

The first meeting between the National Maritime Board Crew Accommodation Committee and the Ministry was arranged to take place on February 21, 1950, with the Under Secretary in the Chair. Attending the meeting from the National Maritime Board were nineteen members representing shipowners and seven representatives of men's unions, viz. the Navigators' and Engineer Officers' Union, the National Union of Seamen, the Mercantile Marine Service Association, the Marine Engineers' Association and the Radio Officers' Union. (As was indicated earlier, committees of the N.M.B. do not necessarily have equal representation from both sides of the industry.)

In opening the meeting, the Under Secretary suggested that they should confine themselves to matters of substance and that drafting points should not be considered at length. The meeting agreed to this course, and proceeded to consider the individual Regulations one by one. Some of the points which were raised by the owners had already been sent by them to the Ministry and the unions in accordance with the usual practice, which enabled the Ministry to give advance thought to their problems before meeting in committee.

One major point which still preoccupied the owners was the

application of the Regulations to ships already in service. They proposed in the preliminary memorandum which they had sent to the Ministry that there should be an explanatory statement in the Regulations that the requirements relating to this should be applied when 'reasonably practicable' and they wanted assurances that the new Regulations would be carried out in a 'reasonable and practicable' manner. At the meeting on February 21st, the Under Secretary suggested that this could be dealt with at the drafting stage.

During the meeting, 81 points were considered. Where agreement was not reached, the points were to be re-considered, and in one case arrangements were made for discussion by one of the shipowners' technical representatives with the Ministry's Principal Surveyor for Tonnage. The Ministry agreed that after reconsidering the points raised, they would send a copy of amendments to the current draft of the Regulations to the N.M.B. The N.M.B. would then consider the points on their side and arrange for special representations to be made on behalf of (1) small ships and day ships[1] and (2) whalers; they would also submit the conclusions of a special committee dealing with galley equipment and ranges.

Follow-up by the Ministry

As had been agreed, the Principal made a list of points for further consideration in the Department. These included the points raised at the meeting on February 21st, with the addition of points made by the Principal Officers at the ports and the professional staff at Headquarters.

He also prepared, from the minutes of the meeting of February 21st, the points which the N.M.B. wished to reconsider internally. These included questions relating to the accommodation of apprentices and to the provision of single rooms for Watchkeeping and Radio Officers, and detailed points on the height and size of beds, provision of oilskin lockers and consideration of standards of cooking equipment.

He also prepared a separate list of the points likely to be raised by the Small Ships Committee of the N.M.B. These covered such things as exemptions from a number of require-

[1] Day ships are ships whose service does not require crews to sleep on board.

ments which would be difficult to carry out on small ships. For example, the provision that steam supply pipes to steam steering gear should not pass through crew accommodation is impracticable on small ships. A provision for ships not provided with mechanical ventilation to be fitted with electric fans would not be possible on many small ships as they had no electricity. In fact the first of these provisions was not applied as it stood to ships of under 500 tons, which were exempted subject to certain safeguards. There was also provision for an exemption from the requirement for an electric fan for ships of under 500 tons. A number of similar points were to be raised for special consideration in respect of small ships at a separate meeting between the Ministry and the N.M.B. Small Ships Committee.

As a result of the consultations so far undertaken, a note was made of points which could usefully be included in the Handbook for Surveyors. For example, it would be necessary to specify desirable standards in respect of water supply, on the grounds that neither a hot water system nor showers might be possible in small ships. It would also be necessary to give guidance on the application of a Regulation which prohibited steam supply pipes from passing through crew accommodation. The reason for this regulation was to guard against the escape of steam and also to avoid the inconvenience of having noisy machinery sited near sleeping-rooms. In the Handbook to Surveyors (published under the title of *Crew Accommodation in Merchants Ships*) advice was given that sleeping-rooms should, where practicable be sited clear of deck machinery particularly steam or oil-driven reciprocating cargo winches or cranes. Where this would not be practicable Surveyors should see the machinery in operation, and be satisfied that all practicable steps had been taken to minimize noise and vibration.

As the consultations continued further practical points of this kind, where guidance to Surveyors was needed on how to apply Regulations, were listed by the Principal. A further list of forty-seven points was drawn up involving amendments to the draft Regulations, either as a result of points agreed in the Department or with the National Maritime Board, all but five of them being points of substance.

For example, one of the draft Regulations provided that

rooms were to be entered from passages provided with permanently attached means of closing and not from the open deck, but the Minister could exempt ships not proceeding to sea from this requirement. The N.M.B. had suggested retaining the 1937 wording, 'the accommodation must be accessible at all times and the entrance must be properly attached', and substituting in the second part the words, 'Cabins generally must be entered from passages and not from the open deck unless the sanction of the Board has been obtained'. At the meeting on February 21st, the Ministry suggested widening the proviso to read 'The Minister may exempt ships if he is satisfied by reason of their size that compliance with this requirement is unreasonable or impracticable'. This was accepted by the meeting. The final version[1] was 'Access to sleeping-rooms, mess rooms, recreation rooms and studies forming part of the crew accommodation shall be obtained from a passageway which shall be provided with a hinged door at any entrance from the open deck. The Minister may exempt any ship from the requirement of this sub-paragraph to the extent that he is satisfied that compliance therewith is unreasonable or impracticable by reason of the size or intended service of the ship.'

Some of the provisions of the first draft had been found by the N.M.B. to be too specific, and it had been agreed that they should be made more flexible. For example, the first draft had specified that every officer should have in his sleeping-room a settee at least six feet long having drawers or lockers underneath. One of the shipowners' representatives said that this should be amended to read that there should be a settee at least six feet long if practicable and the requirement for drawers or lockers underneath should be omitted, and this had been agreed, but was later further modified.[2]

On March 2nd, a meeting was held in the Ministry between the Assistant Secretary, the P.S.T. and the Principal and as a result further points were noted for Departmental reconsideration. These included such matters as ensuring that personal lockers would be secure, providing mirrors for officers, and making sure that provision of a separate sleeping-room for a Chief Cook on a foreign-going vessel of 3,000 tons or over could also include a Chief Steward on a similar vessel.

[1] Regulation 9(2)(c).   [2] See Regulation 18(4)(d).

Ministry Meets N.M.B.'s Small Ships and Day Ships Committee

As has been seen, a number of the provisions in the draft Regulations created difficulties for the owners of small ships. Vessels of less than 500 tons were exempt from the provisions of the Seattle and Geneva Conventions, except that 'where reasonable and practicable' the provisions were to be applied to vessels of between 200 and 500 tons. Before discussing the problems with the N.M.B., a preliminary Departmental meeting was held, attended by the same people as on March 2nd, to consider the applicability of the Regulations to day ships, harbour and esturial craft and very small ships.

Day ships were covered by the Seattle Convention so far as they were of 500 tons and over. The Convention did not stipulate that sleeping accommodation must be provided, but only that where provided it must conform to certain standards. On the other hand, the PST advised that most large day vessels had standard crew accommodation and did not differ materially in design from normal vessels. The meeting thought that it should be possible to make reasonable concessions to the owners without going against the Convention.

As far as very small ships were concerned, the draft Regulations already contained certain concessions with regard to parts of the crew accommodation such as mess rooms and sleeping-rooms, enabling the Minister to vary the requirements. The position of a very small ship, which, because of its function, would not require certain accommodation at all, needed to be clarified. The Department thought that this might be covered by a new clause saying that the requirements to provide a specified type of accommodation should not apply in cases where, in the opinion of the Minister, it was unnecessary by reason of the service of the ship to provide such accommodation in whole or in part.

In preparation for the meeting with the Small Ships and Day Ships Committee of the N.M.B., the Principal prepared a list of points which were likely to be raised. This was taken from the list of points provided for the Ministry by the owners before the full meeting held on February 21st.

Some of these points are as follows: (1) In small ships, it is impossible to exclude steam pipes from rooms used by crew.

The Seattle Convention made any concessions impossible for ships of 500 tons or over, but it was suggested by the Principal that for those under 500 tons there might be a relaxation so long as safety precautions were taken. (2) There was a proposal to change the wording of a clause relating to heating systems, the result of which would have been to prevent the Ministry from exercising any discretion to refuse the use of stoves in vessels of under 500 tons. The Principal suggested that any relaxation in this direction should be resisted because of the danger of fire. (3) There was a possibility that the N.M.B. might ask for a precise definition of 'cold waters', in the clause saying that all ships without mechanical ventilation must be fitted with electric fans except where operating in cold waters. This too the Principal suggested should be resisted, as it would limit the Ministry's ability to interpret the term 'cold waters' flexibly to meet possible special cases.

There were many similar points on topics ranging from the provision of a separate mess room for the Master and Officers on the one hand, and for Petty Officers and ratings on the other; to separate sleeping accommodation for various categories of ships' crews. Where the Convention allowed room for manœuvre on these points the meeting suggested that the Ministry should hear the N.M.B. views and jointly consider them.

The meeting with the N.M.B. took place on March 9th. It was attended by the Under Secretary, the Assistant Secretary, the P.S.T. and the Principal for the Ministry, by five representatives of owners, and by one representative of the National Union of Seamen, two of the Navigators' and Engineer Officers' Union, one of the Marine Engineers' Association, and one of the Radio Officers' Union. These representatives of shipowners and men constituted the Small Ships and Day Ships Committee of the N.M.B.

It was found that the points raised by the N.M.B closely followed those foreshadowed in the preparatory note. For example, the point about the passage of steam pipes through crew quarters in ships of under 500 tons was raised and settled along the lines forecast in the preparatory note. The provision of separate messrooms for officers and crew was raised as a difficulty by one of the N.M.B. Committee, representing owners, and he also said that on very small ships messrooms and living rooms might be combined. It was agreed that there should be a relaxation with regard to separate messrooms for officers and crew for ships of under 500 tons and that there should be a further relaxation allowing messroom and a living room to be combined in ships under 300 tons.[1] On day ships, the Under Secretary explained that the Department had examined the application of the Convention and foresaw no difficulty about complying with it but he suggested a separate meeting between the Ministry and representatives of companies interested in day ships.

The Second Draft

Following this meeting, the Principal drew up further lists of points for reconsideration, which the Assistant Secretary arranged to deal with in instalments by discussion within the Department, after which the resulting suggested amendments could be circulated to the industry. No less than seven instalments of amendments resulted from the various discussions and were circulated as they were prepared to the Under Secretary.

By July 1950, the Principal was able to prepare a consolidated list. He suggested that this should be discussed at a Departmental meeting, after which the current draft of the Regulations could be amended and submitted to the industry. The portions which differed from the previous draft would be underlined. After the industry's comments had been received, an agreed draft should be put in the hands of the Treasury Solicitor. The Ministry had also been promised the N.M.B's views on certain points.

On February 22, 1950, the Ministry had asked the Norwegian Ministry of Commerce and Shipping, who had by that time ratified the Seattle Convention, for a copy of their Regulations and these were sent on March 9th. They were examined by the Principal and on March 31st he drew up a list of a few points which were of interest to the Ministry. One was that the Norwegians had provided for separate accommodation for female personnel, a possibility which had not been mentioned by anyone in this country. Others applied specifically to whaling

[1] See Regulations 19(2) and 19(3).

ships. The Principal suggested that at the Departmental meeting consideration should be given to recommending some of the Norwegian provisions to the industry and he undertook to check the current draft and proposed amendments against the Seattle and Geneva Conventions.

On August 31, 1950, the Assistant Secretary sent copies of the amended draft Regulations to the N.M.B., to other interested branches of the Ministry and to the Principal Officers at the ports. The letter to the N.M.B. said: 'the draft has now been discussed at a series of meetings between representatives of the Department and the Board, and a second draft, copies of which are enclosed, has been prepared to meet the points which were raised. The Minister hopes that the Board will be able to give early consideration to the new draft, and will furnish further comments as soon as possible.'

In addition to the main text of the Regulations, there were three technical Appendices dealing with the provision of a trunked mechanical ventilation system, with deck sheathings, with insulating material for the underside of decks, and with the marking of crew space to show for which class of officer or member of crew they were intended. These had been referred in February, 1950, to the P.S.T. and C.S.S. for their consideration before being sent to the N.M.B. In October, 1950, after receiving them back from the P.S.T., the Principal sent a copy to the Assistant Secretary together with a number of comments, and on November 20th, he sent drafts of these Appendices to the N.M.B. office again with copies to interested branches of the Ministry and to all Principal Officers.

On January 5, 1951, the N.M.B. sent their comments on the second draft of the Regulations. Altogether there were 35 points. The Board were still much concerned with the application of the Regulations to existing ships and again asked for assurances that reasonable arrangements would be specifically provided in both the Regulations themselves and the Instructions to Surveyors.

Another point raised was as follows:

This Regulation stipulates that beds for Chief Officers and Chief or Second Engineers shall be at least 3 feet 6 inches wide. This would be a new requirement for passenger vessels and would be unreasonable and in some cases impracticable. It is not customary for wives to accompany their husbands on passenger liners. The Board agreed to recommend that this clause should be amended to permit beds with a minimum width of 2 feet 9 inches in passenger liners.[1]

A point which the N.M.B. had raised at the earlier meeting but which had been deferred for further consideration was that written complaints should be signed by three members of a crew and not simply by one as was provided in the draft. The N.M.B. now raised this again and pressed the point on the grounds that one troublemaker might become an intolerable nuisance.

The Board suggested that the quickest way to settle all the outstanding points would be to have another meeting with the Ministry.

Ministry Consider N.M.B.'s Comments

Another and final meeting between the Ministry and the N.M.B. was in fact fixed for March 14, 1951, but before it was held the Principal first examined the N.M.B.'s comments and prepared notes on them which he sent to the Assistant Secretary and the P.S.T. on January 19, 1951, suggesting that the three of them should meet to discuss them.

His comment on the position of 'existing ships' was that this had been dealt with in Instructions to Surveyors and to put it again in the Regulations would be unnecessary and would almost certainly be struck out by the lawyers as redundant. On the question of the width of Chief Officers' beds, the Principal suggested that this point should be agreed to. On complaints by members of the crew the Principal's comment was as follows:

I think we should resist this proposal. In the first place, we ought to leave the avenue of complaint open to any individual and take the risk of the procedure being abused. Secondly, it is possible under the Merchant Shipping Acts for a single seaman to voice complaints about food and water, and we really could not justify a departure in this context. Thirdly, as the Under Secretary pointed out at the meeting, three is a high figure on small ships.

[1] See Regulation 17(9)(b).

Before the final meeting with the N.M.B. the Principal arranged a meeting with the professional staff at Headquarters, i.e. the P.S.T. and C.S.S., to consider the draft Regulations.

One point raised by the C.S.S. was the use of the term 'existing ship' in the draft. His comment on this was 'Suggest omission of "existing". What is an existing ship anyway?' The Principal replied that the word 'existing' would probably be struck out by the lawyers but that it was a convenient term to use meanwhile. The remaining points raised by the C.S.S. were mainly technical and were in general accepted.

In order to get further guidance before the final meeting the Principal had a talk with a member of the Shipping Federation about the wording of the Appendices. In a note of February 7, 1951, on this conversation he said that he had received some helpful criticisms.

On February 8th, the Principal minuted the Treasury Solicitor about some points on which he sought advice before the final meeting with the N.M.B. One of these was whether any reference was necessary in the Regulations to the position of 'existing ships'. The Treasury Solicitor, in replying on February 12, 1951, agreed that it was unnecessary to do so.

Meanwhile, owners with ships under construction were keeping an eye on the probable effect of the new Regulations, as also were the Surveyors who would have to apply them. One of the shipowners' representatives on the N.M.B. Crew Accommodation Committee telephoned the Ministry on February 20, 1951 and asked what provisions the Ministry was drawing up about insulation of ships. A tanker was being built at Newcastle upon Tyne and if a certain type of sheathing were insisted upon, it would be very expensive and in his view unnecessary; furthermore it would have to be ripped out if the shell of the ship had to be examined. The Assistant Secretary asked the P.S.T. what advice should be given to this shipowner. On February 21st, the P.S.T. replied that the expensive form of sheathing suggested was not to be a compulsory requirement and suggested that part of the Instructions to Surveyors which had been prepared in draft form should be passed on to the owner to reassure him, and this was done at once.

The internal preparations by the Ministry for the final meeting were almost complete, but in order to ensure that the draft Regulations complied with the Geneva Convention, both the Principal and the Assistant Secretary went through the Convention to ensure that nothing had been missed from the draft Regulations, and a list of points where there was need for further thought or for amendment was prepared on February 26th and sent to the P.S.T.

In order to make sure that all the observations of the N.M.B. were in the Ministry's hands in time to be examined before the meeting on March 14th, a reminder was sent to them on February 28th, asking for a reply to two letters of November and December 1950, to which they had not replied. On March 6th they replied with their further comments, among them the general point that the shipowners' organizations would prefer the technical Appendices not to be in the form of a Statutory Instrument since this might retard development as new techniques became available to the shipbuilders.

Also before the meeting, the Assistant Secretary asked the Principal to find out how many countries had ratified the two Conventions. Norway, France, Sweden, Finland and Bulgaria had ratified the Seattle Convention, of which the first three had each more than a million tons of shipping. The Convention would come into force six months after the ratification by at least seven of certain selected countries, of which four must have more than a million tons of shipping registered.

The Geneva Convention had to be ratified separately, but the same provisions with regard to the number of countries to ratify before it could come into force applied. This Convention had been ratified by Norway, Sweden and Denmark, all of which had over a million tons of shipping.

Final Meeting with N.M.B.

On March 14, 1951, the final meeting with the full Crew Accommodation Committee of the N.M.B. was held. On the question of the application of the Regulations to 'existing ships', it was agreed that the appropriate sections of the Merchant Shipping Act should be reproduced as an Appendix to the Instructions to Surveyors and this was in fact done.

Many of the N.M.B. proposals had already been put before the Ministry by letter and the majority of these were briefly discussed and in the main agreed by the Ministry. The Ministry brought forward a number of points, and most of these also were agreed, or a compromise was reached. An example of such a compromise is recorded as follows:

> We had suggested a separate room where apprentices can study. The N.M.B. made a counter-proposal that 'adequate facilities for quiet study' should be provided.
>
> We reached a compromise settlement on this point to the effect that a separate room should be provided unless the Minister is satisfied that adequate facilities for quiet study exist already.

On the question of complaints from crew, there was considerable discussion before it was eventually agreed that complaints should be accepted from one seaman in ships under 1,000 tons and from three seamen in other ships.[1]

A few points were raised which still needed action but on the whole the preparatory work could be considered finished and the Regulations ready for the lawyers. In the words of the minutes of the final meeting:

> These deliberations finalized the text of the draft Crew Accommodation Regulations apart from the further action listed. These points will be pursued as soon as possible.
>
> The Chairman closed the meeting by thanking the representatives of the N.M.B. for their help and co-operation in assisting the preparation of the draft Regulations. These sentiments were reciprocated for the N.M.B. by Mr X.

On March 22, 1951, the Principal formally submitted the draft Regulations to the Treasury Solicitor asking him to prepare them in legal form and saying that agreements on some points had still to be reached but that these need not hold up the preparations.

PREPARING FINAL TEXT OF REGULATIONS AND HANDBOOK

Some Outstanding Points

On April 10th the Principal wrote to the N.M.B. confirming that the points which had been agreed at the meeting had been incorporated into the text of the Regulations, and enclosing

[1] See Regulation 35(f).

thirty copies for reference. He listed the outstanding points which were still to be settled. He said that the legal draft of the Regulations was being prepared and that when this had been done the text would be sent to the N.M.B. for comments. He also said that the Ministry would send a draft of the Instructions to Surveyors to the Board for their consideration.

On April 26th he wrote to the N.M.B. giving them the Ministry's proposals for settlement of the outstanding points, and on May 25th he sent a reminder asking for an early reply. On May 31st and June 7th the N.M.B. replied but they also raised some new points. On June 13th the Principal commented and suggested that a final reply should be sent to both letters together.

An internal meeting was held on June 29, 1951, attended by the Assistant Secretary, the P.S.T. and an E.O. on the Principal's staff[1] to dispose of the outstanding points on the Regulations. On July 7th, the Principal minuted the Treasury Solicitor with a note of the agreements on the outstanding points. His minute concluded with the following comment:

> I realize, of course, that the drafting of the Statutory Instrument is being suspended at present in view of the discussions about a possible draft Bill,[2] but you may care to have these points in advance of resumption of work.

In a further minute the following day he raised some more points including again the desire of the N.M.B. for a reference to 'existing ships' to be included in the Regulations as well as the Act of 1948. The Treasury Solicitor in his reply of July 13th amplified his comment of February 12th.

> It is quite unnecessary, and I believe entirely without precedent to schedule the text of the governing Act to a Statutory Instrument made thereunder. However, if you or the N.M.B. are publishing a handbook containing these regulations, there would be no objection to reproducing the text as explanatory matter in a footnote, if that were thought to be useful.

On September 3, 1951, the Assistant Secretary wrote to the N.M.B. sending them a copy of the draft of the Instructions to Surveyors, saying that it was proposed to rename this and for

---

[1] In the absence of the Principal.   [2] See above, page 79.

the time being it was being referred to as the Handbook. At the same time he replied to the outstanding comments of the N.M.B. made in their letter of June 7th.

Meanwhile the Treasury Solicitor had been examining the text of the Regulations with a view to preparing it in legal form as a Statutory Instrument, and on November 16, 1951, he sent his draft to the Principal asking how far it fulfilled the intentions of the Regulations. In his minute he said that he was acting on the assumption that the Merchant Shipping Bill would become law.[1]

One problem which he raised was the need for precise definitions and specifications. To quote from his minute:

> In particular, I must ask you to reconsider the Appendices. In Appendices A and B, the reference to 'exhibiting the following properties to the satisfactory degree' is not permissible. Satisfactory to whom? To the owner, the union, the surveyor? Obviously what it means is 'satisfactory to the surveyor or the Minister', and this is not permissible. The Act provides that the requirements shall be prescribed by the Minister in a Statutory Instrument subject to annulment in pursuance of a resolution of either House of Parliament. The Appendices, as drafted, might be construed as an attempt to avoid that provision by enabling the Minister or the Surveyor to lay down the precise requirements outside the Regulations, without the knowledge of Parliament or the public. Accordingly, I must ask you to give me fresh instructions which specify what is required, or the criteria by which the sufficiency of the material, etc., is judged. I shall be glad to discuss this problem further, or indeed any problem arising from my re-draft.

On March 15, 1952, the Principal sent a copy of the Regulations to the Shipbuilding Conference,[2] not for circulation (since they had not yet been legally drafted) but to provide material for answers to questions which might be raised by shipbuilders.

Points on the Draft Handbook

In drawing up the draft Handbook the Ministry had thought of a number of points on the practical working of the Regulations. In particular, there was the question of procedure to be

---

[1] i.e. the Bill which became the Merchant Shipping Act, 1952.
[2] An association of shipbuilding firms.

followed where the Regulations provided that in specific instances the Minister might exempt a particular ship from certain provisions, after consultation with representatives of the owner and seamen concerned.[1]

The Ministry suggested to the N.M.B. on June 9, 1952, that in all these cases time would be saved if the variations from the requirements of the Regulations were discussed in the first instance between the owners and the seafarers' organizations and the agreed points were then sent to the Ministry Surveyor with the crew accommodation plans of the particular ship concerned.

They further suggested that it would often be advantageous if the Surveyor were present at the joint consultation so that, if necessary, he could attempt to reconcile conflicting views on the basis that the requirements of the Regulation should be met as far as was reasonable and practicable; but they pointed out that the final decision would rest with the Ministry.

It had still not been possible to finalize the Regulations in legal form, primarily owing to pressure of work on more urgent Regulations arising out of a Safety of Life at Sea Convention and in a letter of June 14th this was explained to the N.M.B. by the Assistant Secretary. He also said that it was hoped that the Regulations would be made and signed by the Minister in the autumn of 1952. At first it had been intended that there should be an interval of six months between the date of the making of the Regulations and of their coming into force, but in view of the delay the Ministry proposed that this interval should be only three months. The object of the interval was to allow the owners and builders ample time to familiarize themselves with the contents of the Regulations.

The comment of the N.M.B. on the proposed method of consultation was as follows:

Consultation with shipowners' and seafarers' organizations.
Whilst the owners feel that the method of consultation suggested by the Ministry can be adopted in principle, they wish it to be clearly understood by all concerned that it will be at the option of the shipowner whether or not he initiates—or takes part in—the local consultations suggested. . . .

[1] e.g. Regulation 16(3)(f) relating to the number of ratings who might sleep in one room.

Similarly the owners commented that instead of the proposed three months interval six months would be far preferable.

In the event, in the Handbook (now entitled *Crew Accommodation in Merchant Ships*) no reference was made to the details of the method of consultation, but the Ministry's Instructions to Surveyors[1] did propose the method already suggested. It was, however, pointed out that the onus for consultation was laid by the Act on the Ministry and owners could not be required to consult the unions.

The First Legal Draft

On August 26th, Lloyds Daily List published the information that the International Labour Office had received the necessary number of seven ratifications[2] and that the Convention would therefore come into force from January 29, 1953. The Under Secretary commented in a minute:

> It would be most unfortunate if this Convention were to come into force before the United Kingdom had ratified. We ought to be one of the countries which apply the Convention requirements at the outset. Can we overcome the drafting difficulties and make our new Regulations effective on 29th January, 1953? The industry may have to accept shorter notice than we had hoped to give.

The Treasury Solicitor had now been able to give more attention to the legal drafting of the Regulations and had raised a point about the specification of exemptions from the Regulations in the Regulations themselves, which seemed to him illogical since general power for the Minister to grant exemption was contained in the Act. He therefore suggested that these discretionary exemption arrangements should be transferred from the Regulations to the Handbook.

On this the Principal minuted the Assistant Secretary that the main difficulty was that during the Committee debate in the House of Commons the Minister stated that the exemptions would be specified in the Regulations. In reply the Assistant

---

[1] Not a published document but a set of instructions for internal use.

[2] Denmark, France, Norway and Sweden each with over one million tons of shipping, together with Finland, Ireland and Portugal.

Secretary minuted the Under Secretary that it had always been the intention to specify the exemptions in the Regulations as had been done in other cases; there was too the advantage that there would be a clear indication of the cases in which the powers could be exercised and less of an excuse for shipowners to plead for exemption from other provisions.

The Under Secretary replied:

> We must mention the exemptions in the Regulations except in those cases where an exemption will be infrequent and we do not want to stimulate applications. . . .

On December 13, 1952, the Treasury Solicitor sent the legal draft of the Regulations to the Principal and said that he would like to discuss certain passages with him and the P.S.T.

The legal draft was sent to the N.M.B. with a covering letter of February 3, 1953. It will be seen that it had not been possible to get the Regulations made by January 29, 1953, the date when the Seattle Convention (No. 75) came into force; and in fact the Regulations were not made until July 1953.

With the letter of February 3rd to the N.M.B. went a list of points of differences between the legal draft and the lay version of August 1950. The letter also explained that the phraseology was in many cases necessarily different because of the legal force of certain terms. It also explained that some of the points had been re-marshalled so as to bring together in the Regulations all points concerning a particular aspect of crew accommodation, thus making the Regulations more logical. Once again the Ministry asked for the Board's comments on the draft as rephrased in legal terminology.

On February 12th, the legal draft was sent by the Principal to the Ministry of Labour with a request that their legal advisers should examine it to ensure that it would give effect to the provisions of the I.L.O. Convention No. 92. In their reply of March 14th, the Ministry of Labour made a number of comments but suggested that it would make things easier if the Ministry of Transport could indicate in respect of each Article of the Convention the particular draft Regulation which gave effect to it.

The Problem of Bringing the Regulations into Force

On February 14th, the Treasury Solicitor, in a minute to the Principal, raised the question of bringing the Regulations into force. He said:

> The Ministry of Labour, we understand, will not ratify the I.L.O. Convention until the Regulations are made or are on the point of being made, and under the Act you cannot bring the Sections into force before the Convention applies to the U.K. unless it is the wish of (all?) organizations representing the British owners and seamen that you should do so. The simplest procedure would therefore be—
>
> (1) To agree with the Ministry of Labour a date on which ratification is to be deposited.
>
> (2) Upon receipt of telegraphic confirmation that it has been deposited, to make an Order bringing the Sections into force on a date six months thence (the date on which the Convention will apply to the U.K.).
>
> (3) Immediately thereafter, to make the Regulations expressing them to come into operation on the date mentioned above. It would be best to agree the whole of this procedure with the Ministry of Labour, getting their prior agreement to the proof which is to be signed on behalf of the Minister.

Another meeting was fixed between the Ministry and the N.M.B. to discuss the legal draft of the Regulations, to be held on April 29, 1953.

On March 26th the Principal wrote to the Ministry of Labour explaining the suggested procedure for bringing the Regulations into force. This procedure was not the normal one, but resulted from certain provisions of the Merchant Shipping Act of 1948.

The Ministry of Labour replied on April 7th and pointed out that the Ministry of Transport procedure would not be possible, or rather not without considerable delay. The reason was that the Merchant Shipping Act had referred both to Convention No. 75 and to another Convention No. 68 concerning Food and Catering for Crews on Board Ship, and to follow the procedure suggested by the Ministry of Transport and ratify the Crew Accommodation Convention would mean only a partial ratification and would not therefore fulfil the conditions laid down in the Act, which were that the Regulations would come into force only when both Conventions had been ratified and had come into operation. Although the United Kingdom could ratify the Food and Catering Convention at the same time, this would not have the effect of bringing it into force, since there were not enough ratifications by other countries of that Convention and no immediate prospect that there would be sufficient within a short time. The Ministry of Labour therefore suggested that either some way should be found of treating the two Conventions separately; or the provision in the Act should be used which would permit the Regulations to be brought into force before the Conventions applied to the United Kingdom if it was the wish of 'such organization or organizations as appear to him (the Minister) to be representative of both owners of British Ships and seamen employed therein'. This was the procedure which was in fact followed.

The first problem set by the Ministry of Labour was to ensure that in fact the Regulations expressed the intention of the Convention. A detailed schedule specifying each Article of the Convention and showing in which Regulation its intention was carried out was prepared in the Ministry of Transport in March 1953. In a number of cases there seemed to be doubt about whether the Regulations complied with the Convention. For example, Article 11 (8) of the Convention was paralleled by Regulation 19 (2) and the comment was made by the Ministry of Transport: 'The Convention says mess rooms shall be located apart from (at a distance from ?) the sleeping rooms. The Regulations say "No mess room shall be combined with a sleeping room". Has this the same meaning?'

On April 1st, a meeting was held at the Ministry of Transport between the representative of the Treasury Solicitor's Department in the Ministry, the Principal, the P.S.T. and the H.E.O., to consider comments on the draft Regulations made by the Ministry of Labour in their letter of March 14th. As a result of this meeting, a list of amendments and of points requiring further consideration was drawn up by the Principal on April 10, 1953.

The Legal Draft Discussed with the N.M.B.

In preparation for the meeting to be held between the Ministry of Transport and the Crew Accommodation Committee of the N.M.B., the owners' side of the N.M.B. Committee asked their members to prepare a list of points on the legal draft of the Regulations. They intended to send these to the Ministry in advance of the meeting which was to be held on April 29, 1953, but as this proved impossible they sent the Ministry a list of suggested points which had been circulated by the owners' side of the N.M.B. Committee for their special consideration.

This was done on April 17th when the owners' side also promised to put the points into a logical order and send them to the seafarers' side of the Committee. There were 75 comments, many of them points of detail or of drafting but there were a few comments of importance such as one dealing with the application of the Regulations to certain categories of vessels which were on the whole non-sea-going.

On April 18th, the Principal sent the N.M.B. a list of the amendments which were proposed as a result of the comparison of the Regulations with the Geneva Convention No. 92 and asked for the Board's comments. This list was sent by the owners' side of the N.M.B. Committee to their members; they said that as there had been no time for detailed study, members of the Committee were asked to raise any points arising from it at the meeting on April 29th.

A lengthy brief was prepared by the Principal for the Ministry representatives at the meeting on April 29th. The owners' points were examined one by one and noted either to be conceded, resisted, or clarified.

For example, one point raised by the owners was that in the old draft the Regulations were to apply to certain classes of ships, e.g. non-sea-going ships and certain small passenger ships, only if the owners desired to make them applicable; but in the new draft these classes of ships were brought within the scope of the Regulations with power for the Minister to exempt them if it seemed unreasonable to require compliance.

The owners wanted an undertaking that the accommodation would be exempted in so far as the shipowner desired that it should be. The Principal's note on this read:

This point should be resisted.

We are prevented by the terms of Art. 1 of the Convention from giving any such undertaking in respect of any ship which goes to sea.

By dealing with these classes of ships as formerly proposed in the old draft we would be asked to give authoritative guidance as to which individual ships could be regarded as sea-going for the purpose of the Regulations. We have no authority to give such an interpretation as this is a matter which can only finally be decided by the Courts.

Should these vessels be omitted from the Regulations there would be still left the difficult question of whether or not they are sea-going. If sea-going (and presumably any voyage to sea would render them sea-going) they would require to comply with the Sixth Schedule of the Merchant Shipping Act of 1894. Difficulty has been experienced in determining what are the requirements of the Sixth Schedule, and it would be better for all concerned to know exactly where they stand. It would be simpler if the owners would agree to be brought into the Regulations and to agree with the Minister a code which would apply to their ships in this category.

Many ships in this category would escape from many of the requirements of the Regulations simply because their crews do not sleep or eat on board.

At the meeting on April 29, 1953, the Ministry were represented by the Assistant Secretary (in the chair), the Principal, the P.S.T., and an H.E.O. and an E.O. from the Principal's branch. The chairman said that it was hoped to finalize the Crew Accommodation Regulations so that they could be made on July 1, 1953, and come into effect six months later. It was also hoped to publish the Handbook at the same time as the Regulations were made.

One important point which was settled was that the industry agreed to the proposal to bring the Regulations into force in advance of ratification of Convention No. 68 on Food and Catering on Board Ship. The chairman then apologized for the amount of detail which had to be discussed, explaining that this was 'very largely due to the fact that the Ministry's legal advisers had found themselves unable to accept, as not being sufficiently precise, many of the terms which had been used in the earlier drafts'. It was agreed by the meeting that the procedure should be for them to consider the points raised by the owners; other points would be dealt with as they arose.

The minutes of the meeting make detailed references to a large number of points discussed, and show a fairly even balance between agreement by the Ministry with the owners' points and the owners with the Ministry's points. On the point about small ships (page 102 above), the owners agreed to withdraw their comments after the Ministry had explained their point of view. The representatives of the seafarers had few comments to make.

At the close of the meeting, friendly remarks were made about the spirit in which the discussions had taken place. The minutes read: the chairman 'concluded the meeting by saying that it was probably the last meeting of this kind on crew accommodation, (and) he wished to thank the Board for their patience and constructive help. Mr X on behalf of the owners thanked the Ministry for an interesting and happy association and said there had always been the fullest co-operation from all three sides. Mr Y said that on behalf of the seafarers, he wished to be associated with Mr X's remarks.'

Once again the Assistant Secretary sent a copy of the legal draft of the Regulations to the Shipbuilding Conference explaining that there would be a few changes as a result of the last meeting with the N.M.B. He also explained that the Regulations were not likely to come into force until January, 1954, six months after they would, if all went well, be made, and also that the Handbook, giving guidance to the application of the Regulations, would, it was hoped, be issued shortly after the Regulations were made.

Final Amendments: The Statutory Instrument Made

Lists of amendments arising out of the discussions at the meeting with the N.M.B. on April 29, 1953, were drawn up by the Principal and an internal meeting at the Ministry was held between the representative of the Treasury Solicitor, the P.S.T., the Principal and the H.E.O. on May 11th to arrive at final amendments.

By May 20, 1953, the Assistant Secretary was able to record that he had told the Ministry of Labour that the new Regulations would in all probability be published on July 1, 1953. The Ministry of Labour promised to arrange for their solicitors to make comments as quickly as possible; all the administrative people would at that time be in Geneva, which might make consultation with them difficult.

On June 5th the Principal sent a list of amendments to the N.M.B., as agreed at the meeting of April 29th, for circulation to the N.M.B. members.

On June 8th, the Principal wrote to the Ministry of Labour in reply to their letters of March 14th and April 7th. The letter agreed that the power to make the Regulations in advance of the Conventions coming into force should be used and included a list of amendments as finally agreed between the Ministry of Transport and the N.M.B., and a note showing how each Article of the Geneva Convention No. 92 was carried into effect by the Regulations.

It also pressed the Ministry of Labour to consider the draft Regulations as a matter of urgency, as the Ministry of Transport wished them to be made on July 1, 1953.

As the time was approaching for the Regulations to be made law, the shipowners were anxious that all their members should be fully aware of their obligations under them. They therefore prepared a draft circular to be sent to owners informing them of the reason for the new legislation and of its effect, together with a copy of the Statutory Instrument embodying the Regulations; the circular also explained the purpose of the Handbook and gave an undertaking to send one copy as soon as it was published. On May 29th this draft was sent to the Ministry for comments, and on June 10th the Principal replied with some suggested amendments; in particular, that there should be a reference to the fact that owners should get in touch with the Ministry at as early a stage as possible where any question of exemption from the Regulations was likely to be raised. A paragraph on these lines was in fact included in the circular as sent to the owners by the Shipping Federation.

By June 17, 1953, it was possible for the Assistant Secretary to minute the Deputy Secretary for the Shipping Group of Divisions, attaching, for the Minister's approval, the final draft of the Merchant Shipping (Crew Accommodation) Regulations, subject to final confirmation of the wording of one or two points and to possible further minor amendments as a result of final legal scrutiny.

He submitted an explanatory statement outlining the origin and purpose of the Regulations, and concluded:

> The Minister's approval is accordingly sought to the making of (1) the Regulations submitted (subject to any minor amendments which may be found to be necessary) and expressed to come into operation on 1st January, 1954 and (2) an Order bringing Sections 1 to 4 of the Merchant Shipping Act 1948 into operation for the purpose of making the Regulations, on 1st July next.

On June 20th the Principal asked the Clerk of Printing and Stationery to print the Regulations in the form of a Statutory Instrument. On the same day he also wrote to the Ministry of Labour, sending a copy of the final text of the Regulations and asking for any comments within a day or two.

Even at this late date one or two further suggestions were arriving at the Ministry; the N.M.B. wrote on June 19th, and again on the 22nd and the Shipping Federation also wrote on June 18th. These points were settled either by telephone conversations or by additions to the Handbook.

By June 26, 1953, the Assistant Secretary was able to send a minute to the Deputy Secretary (Shipping) to say that all the minor points had been disposed of. He also said that he had discussed and agreed one or two points on the Regulations by telephone with the Ministry of Labour representatives who were all at the time in Geneva, and that he understood from the Minister's Private Secretary that the Minister had received a minute from the Deputy Secretary about the Regulations and that he would be available to sign them. He also attached, for the Deputy Secretary to see, a copy of the Commencement Order and a copy of a draft Press Notice. The Press Notice had been sent to the Ministry of Labour people in Geneva and they were to send their comments.

On June 29th the Assistant Secretary recorded a note of a discussion on the telephone with Ministry of Labour representatives in Geneva. One or two points had been raised by the Ministry of Labour but they had agreed that the Regulations should go ahead and be signed in their form as finally drafted.

On June 19th, the Deputy Secretary (Shipping) had minuted

the Permanent Secretary and put forward the Regulations for the Minister's approval, and on June 24th the Permanent Secretary formally minuted the Minister, referring to the Deputy Secretary's minute and asking for the Minister's approval. This was given with congratulations for all concerned, on June 27th.

The Regulations were laid on the table of the House on July 2nd and subject to negative resolution, that is, they would be automatically passed unless Parliament resolved otherwise within a period of forty days from the date on which they were laid.

A number of steps had to be taken following the making of the Statutory Instrument. The sealed authenticated Statutory Instruments, 1036 of 1953, signed by the Minister and 1035 of 1953 (the Commencement Order) signed by an Under Secretary, were deposited in the Ministry Strong Room, and a Press Notice was issued on July 6th by the Ministry of Transport.

On July 7th a memorandum was sent to Principal Officers and Surveyors enclosing copies of the two Statutory Instruments, and briefly stating their significance. It also said that the Handbook would be sent as soon as possible, and that there would be a notice drawing the attention of ships' Masters to the provisions of the Regulations and a further minute giving advice to Surveyors on the application of the Regulations by them.

On July 27th, the Minister of Transport was asked in the House of Commons which organizations he had consulted with regard to the compilation of Statutory Instrument 1036 and whether the final draft was prepared with their full agreement and the Minister was able to reply that the Regulations were made in consultation with the National Maritime Board and with their full agreement and that the National Maritime Board was fully representative of both the shipowners and the officers and men of the Merchant Navy.

THE PROBLEM OF LIGHTING STANDARDS

Standards too High

The main narrative has been taken to the point where the Regulations were finally made. But the process of administration is not fixed and static, and the publication of the Statutory Instrument was not the end of discussions about the problems of crew accommodation. The following account is an example of such a discussion.

The Regulations were drawn up to come into force six months after they had been made, that is, on January 1, 1954. During this period owners and builders were able to study the provisions of these new Regulations and consider their practical implications, especially for building.

On December, 3, 1953, one of the shipping companies wrote to the Ministry that in their opinion the rules laid down a standard of lighting in excess of what was really necessary. They said they had compared the requirements with the standards on a ship recently delivered to them and had concluded that no advantage would result from a rigid adherence to the rules as they stood. For example, the illumination of alleyways and companionways would be quite satisfactory at 50 per cent of that quoted in the rules; the rating for lighting stores was very much in excess of anything they had installed in the past and found quite acceptable; and in crew accommodation as a whole they had concentrated on ensuring satisfactory lighting at key points, such as washbasins, etc. rather than on obtaining a high level of illumination throughout.

They therefore suggested that consideration should be given to a reduction of the present standards for alleyways, companionways, stores and sanitary accommodation, and that Surveyors should be given latitude to accept lower levels in other accommodation so long as a proper level of illumination was found at points such as writing desks or tables. Their immediate concern was over two ships due to be completed in the first half of 1954 for which detailed instructions to the shipbuilders were needed without delay.

Similar representations were made to the Ministry by other shipowners. Two members of the owners' side of the N.M.B. had called at the Ministry on November 6, 1953, and made the same points. In a minute to the P.S.T. the Principal said that the Assistant Secretary had agreed that it might be necessary to inform ship Surveyors that the full standards of lighting need not be insisted on if the Surveyor was satisfied that the lighting was adequate. The Minute recorded that the P.S.T. was intending to accumulate further data and consider whether the lighting requirements should be modified in any way.

Part of the data consisted of a memorandum prepared by one of the owners' representatives on the N.M.B. which gave the results of lighting tests carried out on a newly built tanker. A ship which was considered to be a typical example of modern tonnage was chosen for the tests. Selected accommodation, representing each type, was chosen and light meter readings were taken and compared with the Ministry's requirements. The memorandum concluded that the general impression was that the lighting as fitted would not comply with the impending Regulations.

As a result of reconsideration by the P.S.T. it was decided that Surveyors should be instructed generally to accept a less rigid standard than that laid down in the Regulations. In a letter of December 5, 1953, to the firm which had raised the question in its letter of December 3rd, the P.S.T. said that the Ministry would agree to the standards they suggested, and he also asked one or two further questions about the lighting of particular spaces, e.g. shower spaces.

On the question of the application of the rules to ships currently under construction, the P.S.T. referred the firm to a paragraph in the Handbook which permitted acceptance by surveyors of fittings and equipment already purchased.

The owners replied on December 9th; on the lighting of shower spaces, they said that their general practice was to fit lights outside the entrance to the showers, but across the entrance to the showers were transparent plastic curtains which let plenty of light into the shower space, and yet prevented water splashing on to the light fitting.

In order to ensure that all Surveyors understood that the Ministry were prepared to accept a less rigid standard of light than that prescribed in the Regulations an instruction was issued to the Principal Officers and Surveyors at the ports. The instructions gave detailed guidance on new standards which would be regarded as satisfactory during the interim period before any revision to the Regulations could be brought into effect, and was issued on December 12, 1953.

In the interim period before the revised lighting standards came into force, the Surveyors were asked to send plans showing the proposed lighting standards of vessels under construction to the P.S.T. at Headquarters. The Principal notified the Shipping Federation and also the Employers' Association of Liverpool, who had raised similar points about the stringency of the standards in the Regulations, that for the time being Surveyors had been instructed not to reject plans showing standards below those of the new Regulations but to submit particulars of them to the P.S.T. at Headquarters.

Discussions with Shipowners

As a result of those representations, the Ministry arranged a meeting to discuss the problem with representatives of the owners. This took place on January 13, 1954. At this meeting, one of the owners' representatives said that a full examination and investigation made independently by several shipowners had shown that the Regulation requirements went further than they realized when they agreed to them. These views had been co-ordinated and set out in a statement which was circulated at the meeting. This statement listed the ways in which the lighting values specified in the Regulations were considered to be too high, and put forward a suggested revised scale of values.

The P.S.T. then commented at the meeting on the ship-owners' statement and agreed that at some points, such as passageways, lower values might be adequate. After some general discussion of what should constitute adequate lighting, the Chairman (the Assistant Secretary), suggested that it might be best to deal with the various parts of the crew accommodation in turn. This plan was adopted and a revised value was agreed for sleeping rooms, messrooms and recreation rooms, and a modified standard for sanitary accommodation. It was decided that hospital wards and store rooms would be further considered before a decision was reached.

The Principal mentioned that it would be necessary to consult the unions before any revision of the Regulations was made. He also suggested that it might be necessary to give a practical demonstration. The owners said that they were sure that the unions would accept the revised standards, and that there would be no difficulty in arranging a practical demonstration; one of the owners volunteered the help of his company in this.

Another owner asked whether in cases where a plan had been approved and it was later found that the resulting lighting failed to reach Regulation standard, the Ministry would insist on the standard being attained. The P.S.T. pointed out that approval of the plan was subject to inspection at the ship. It must also be realized that the choice of the criterion to be applied, viz. a foot-candle standard, meant the same thing: such a regulation could only be satisfied by actual examination of the completed work by use of a light-meter.

Following the meeting, the P.S.T. prepared a re-draft of the Regulations. In an accompanying memorandum of February 2, 1954, he suggested three different methods of taking light measurements according to the purpose of the lighting. The memorandum also laid down standards in terms of foot candles for each part of the crew accommodation, showing by which of the three methods each should be measured.

On February 11th the Assistant Secretary sent a copy of this memorandum to the Secretary of the Shipping Federation and said that the Ministry proposed sending it to the N.M.B. so that both sides of the industry could express their views on it, but before this was done he would be grateful to know whether he saw any objection to this.

The Secretary of the Shipping Federation was not in favour of the procedure suggested in the memorandum and he called at the Ministry to put forward an alternative version, which followed the method of measurement of the original Regulations but included higher values in accordance with the Ministry's specifications in their revision. During his discussion at the Ministry it was agreed that a revised draft, with certain amendments raising the lighting values, should be sent to the Treasury Solicitor for re-writing in legal form.

Revised Proposals Discussed with the N.M.B.

The Principal therefore sent the Treasury Solicitor a draft of a revised Regulation 11 (6), based on a modified version of the P.S.T.'s memorandum. The actual light values proposed were in some cases slightly higher than those put forward by the Secretary of the Shipping Federation.

On April 13, 1954, the Treasury Solicitor sent his suggested re-draft, in legal form, to the Principal. As both he and the P.S.T. had a few comments, the Principal arranged a meeting of the three of them to discuss the draft, after which the Treasury Solicitor again re-drafted the Regulation. Finally this re-draft was again discussed with the Principal and the P.S.T.

A further point on this Regulation was raised by the Principal in a memorandum. He pointed out that the Regulation required every part of the crew accommodation except drying rooms, lockers and store rooms to be properly lighted by natural light with a few specific exceptions.

But for a cargo ship this would mean having the accommodation on the sides of the ship, with a consequent waste of space. In fact laundries (where they existed) and pantries were commonly placed on the middle line of the ship rather than at the sides where they would take daylight from other more important spaces. He suggested that for ships begun after January 1, 1954, it would be difficult to secure exemption under the existing powers in the Regulations and in any case it seemed absurd to have to go through the formalities of consultation on such a trivial point in every case in which it arose. He therefore suggested amending the Regulations to give specific exemption for laundries and pantries.

These and other proposed points were put to the N.M.B. by the Principal on June 25, 1954, after the representative of the Shipping Federation had agreed to this course, and a meeting was arranged for September 17th between the Ministry and the N.M.B. The N.M.B. sent the Ministry in advance of that meeting the comments of the shipowners' side of the Board. These included a number of detailed points, but there was also the general comment that there was still some feeling that the lighting standards were high and that a number of modern vessels, some still building and nearly completed, where the lighting was undoubtedly good, would not in all cases entirely comply with the proposals.

The meeting on September 17, 1954, was attended by thirteen members of the shipowners' side and five members of the unions' side of the N.M.B. with the Assistant Secretary in the chair, and also, as representatives of the Ministry, the P.S.T., the Principal and an H.E.O. of the Marine (Crews) Division. The meeting examined the amendments put forward by the Ministry in advance, one by one. Agreement was reached either on the Ministry's amendments as drafted or on modifications of them.

Amending Regulations

After reaching agreement the next step was for a Statutory Instrument to be prepared to give effect to these changes.

On September 20th, the Principal sent the Treasury Solicitor a note of the suggested amendments, asking him to furnish the Ministry with a draft of a Statutory Instrument making the necessary amendments to the Merchant Shipping (Crew Accommodation) Regulations 1953, and this was sent on November 2nd.

In order to ensure that the Ministry of Labour had no objections the Principal wrote to them on November 5th explaining the position. In their reply of November 11, 1954, the Ministry of Labour said that they had consulted their Legal Department, who had said that in the light of the Geneva Convention No. 92 they could see no objection to the proposals.

The Principal also wrote to the Dock and Harbour Authorities Association, the Docks and Inland Waterways Board of Management, and the British Transport Commission explaining the reason for the amending Statutory Instrument. None of these bodies raised any objections to the amendments.

In submitting the draft to the Under Secretary for the Minister's approval on November 15th, the Assistant Secretary explained that the main amendment was concerned with lighting. This arose because the existing lighting requirement had been found to be excessive and much too onerous. The amending Regulations provided for a much lower general illumination and for higher illumination at key points.

He said that it was proposed that the new Regulations should come into force on the day following the day of laying them before Parliament, this being the usual procedure where as in this case, the Regulations had been agreed by those affected. He added that in fact, by agreement, the requirements were already being put into effect administratively. The Regulations were approved on December 6th and signed by the Minister on December 13th.

It had been suggested by the Under Secretary that rather than bring these amendments into effect one day after they had been laid on the Table of the House, there should be a fortnight's interval, to allow time for copies to be made available to those concerned, and this had been done. The Parliamentary Branch noted on the file that the Regulations were presented to Parliament on December 17, 1954.

As soon as the Statutory Instrument had been signed, the Principal prepared a draft Press Notice briefly explaining that the amendments had been made by the Minister, and setting out their purpose and saying that copies could be obtained from Her Majesty's Stationery Office.

He also wrote on December 17, 1954, to the Dock and Harbour Authorities' Association, the British Transport Commission, the Docks and Inland Waterways Board of Management, the N.M.B. and the Shipping Federation and the Shipbuilding Conference, sending them copies of the Statutory Instrument. He also sent copies to the Supervisor of Nautical Services, Ottawa, the Department of Industry and Commerce, Dublin, the Department of Shipping and Fuel, Melbourne, the Office of the High Commissioner for South Africa in London, the Ministry of Labour and National Service and the Home Office.

In order to ensure that the Principal Officers and Surveyors were fully informed about developments, the Principal prepared a suggested memorandum to be circulated to them and agreed it with the P.S.T. This memorandum explained the effect of the new Statutory Instrument.

CONCLUSION

The Case Study and Administrative Problems

With the coming into force of the 1953 Regulations it may be said that a further chapter was closed in the history of the provision of acceptable accommodation for crews of merchant ships. It will be clear from the preceding narrative that this does not mean that nothing further need be done for another thirty years; but in the nature of things a major revision and overhaul of existing provisions such as followed the Seattle

Conference of 1946 is not likely to take place very often. It is in the light of this situation that we should consider the lessons to be drawn from this case study, and its value for gaining an insight into the processes of administration.

The most obvious point arises from the contrast which Crew Accommodation Regulations present with the other study in this volume. The building of new roads is an activity which, in present circumstances, is going on all the time and simultaneously in different parts of the country. However much each individual case may differ in detail there is therefore a basic sequence of operations which must be followed in every case, and it is this routine which, particularly in the case of land acquisition, provides the opportunity for introducing the most economical methods of administration, e.g. by the use of stock forms.

But the case of crew accommodation provides a very different set of administrative problems. Here the emphasis is on the particular conditions in a particular industry for which provision must be made. Moreover, the angle of approach is different from that in the other case. For here we are examining not examples of administrative work within an agreed statutory framework but rather the process by which that frame-work itself is created or at least revised.

The effect of this, as was noted in the Introduction, is that we are here studying the work of (to use Civil Service terms) the Administrative and Professional classes rather than the Executive and Professional. This at once raises a point of great interest and controversy. In this country, in contrast to many others, the responsibility for policy-making decisions rests on the Administrative Class, and the Professional Classes are, formally at least, in the position of advisers and not policy-makers. Thus we find the Principal (and to some extent the Assistant Secretary) handling correspondence, arranging meetings and above all drafting, commenting and re-writing, with the P.S.T. playing the role, as it were, of his right-hand man, making suggestions, drawing up technical memoranda, commenting on his comments and clearly influencing but not actually taking the final decision on such questions as whether to make or accept amendments.

Is this the best system? Much of the Regulations is concerned with technical matters; there are many references to such things as 'thermostatically controlled calorifiers' and 'trunked mechanical ventilation systems', but even more than that, the whole emphasis is on precise specification of the type, design and construction of the various aspects of crew accommodation which are dealt with. Clearly, on matters of this kind, the Professional rather than the Administrator is better able to appreciate the significance of variations and alterations. But the other side of the picture is that somebody must ensure that all the details not only hang together but conform to the general policy which has been adopted. Should the Administrator or the Professional be the man who has the last word?

Arguments on this question will no doubt continue for a long time. But here at least we have some important evidence of how the system works in practice in the middle of the twentieth century. On the one hand, it can certainly be said that so far as crew accommodation was concerned the system worked smoothly and successfully; on the other hand, some may feel that it tends to delay action and to make negotiations longer and more cumbersome than they need be. This case study provides some data for considering the question further.

Closely linked with the problems of Administrative versus Professional expertise is the question of how the negotiations were conducted. Crew accommodation is a favourable subject for negotiation in the sense that there is a large measure of basic agreement on what needs to be done by all the parties most closely concerned. The chief object of negotiation was therefore to arrive, frequently by a process of compromise, at agreement on specific detail. To this end the techniques of both formal and informal consultation were employed and rarely could there be said to be a clash over a point of major principle. Perhaps the nearest approach to such a clash was over the question of 'existing ships' but even here it was rather the manner of application than the principle which was chiefly at issue.

Much of this situation may of course be explained by the history of the regulation of crew accommodation, and in particular by the fact that to a large degree the Ministry's task was to guide the industry as a whole along lines which the best part of it was already following. But it might be argued that a situation of this kind called for rather different techniques and perhaps a rather different type of negotiator than a more controversial situation where the virtues of patient diplomacy are most readily seen to be needed. This then is a further aspect of the argument over the Professional versus the Administrator which this case illuminates.

We are therefore here concerned with the intricacies of negotiation and nothing perhaps is more striking about this case than the painstaking way in which argument and counter-argument are used in an endeavour to be certain that nothing is left to chance and that every detail is agreed by everybody concerned in the negotiations. Thus, it is not simply a chair which is specified in the Regulations but 'a chair with arm rests', not just a wardrobe but 'a wardrobe at least 5 feet 6 inches in height and 460 square inches in internal sectional area'. Such detail is not mere pedantry but an integral part of the way in which the idea of reasonable and adequate accommodation has evolved. Still less is it the product of the bureaucratic mind of Whitehall, as the casual reader of the Regulations might be tempted to think, but an attempt by those who are going to be most affected by the Regulations to be as specific as possible about the minimum standard acceptable. The key figure in all this of the Principal will be apparent, for on him falls the donkey-work.

One final point; if we ask whether all this time-consuming work is really necessary we raise a question of vital concern to the working of democratic processes. For if we believe that it is better to persuade than to compel, then we must accept that, particularly in a situation where three parties are involved, to say nothing of the international link, many words must be written and spoken before final agreement is reached. In a sense, but perhaps to varying degrees, this is the main lesson to be learned from both cases presented here.

GEORGE ALLEN & UNWIN LTD

London: 40 Museum Street, W.C.1

Auckland: 24 Wyndham Street
Bombay: 15 Graham Road, Ballard Estate, Bombay 1
Bridgetown: P.O. Box 222
Buenos Aires: Escritorio 454–459, Florida 165
Calcutta: 17 Chittaranjan Avenue, Calcutta 13
Cape Town: 68 Shortmarket Street
Hong Kong: 44 Mody Road, Kowloon
Ibadan: P.O. Box 62
Karachi: Karachi Chambers, McLeod Road
Madras: Mohan Mansions, 38c Mount Road, Madras 6
Mexico: Villalongin 32–10, Piso, Mexico 5, D.F.
Nairobi: P.O. Box 4536
New Delhi: 13–14 Asaf Ali Road, New Delhi 1
Ontario: 81 Curlew Drive, Don Mills
Philippines: 7 Waling-Waling Street, Roxas District,
Quezon City
São Paulo: Caixa Postal 8675
Singapore: 36c Prinsep Street, Singapore 7
Sydney: N.S.W.: Bradbury House, 55 York Street
Tokyo: 10 Kanda-Ogawamachi, 3-Chome, Chiyoda-Ku

MARJORIE OGILVY-WEBB

THE GOVERNMENT EXPLAINS

A Study of the Information Services

Demy 8vo

28*s. net*

An informed public is the basis of a sound democracy. Public authorities must publicize their work if they are to carry out their duties effectively. But the dividing line between information and propaganda is finely drawn, and public authorities must be on their guard against mis-use of public relations techniques. This study examines the way in which the central government information services have developed within the British constitution as a valuable supplement to the more traditional channels of communication of parliament and the Press.

The book traces the growth of government information services from tentative beginnings in the late nineteenth century, through two world wars—the second, in particular, providing the impetus for rapid growth—to the firmly established public relations organization which exists today. At the apex of this organization is the Minister responsible for co-ordinating information policy, and particular attention is given to the development and growth of the co-ordinating role at both the ministerial and official level.

The study describes the structure and work of the Information Divisions, and discusses the functions of the Central Office of Information in providing them with the professional and technical services they require. In 1949, a new Information Officer Class was created. The book describes the discussions which led to its formation, analyses its form and structure, and examines its relationship with the other Treasury Classes.

The government's public relations are not confined to information officers. For the ordinary citizen the main channel of communication with government is through personal contact with the individual official, on the telephone or by letter. Public relations training for all civil servants who meet the public is therefore of the greatest importance. The study illustrates the methods used in the training of lower grades in the Post Office, the Ministry of Labour, and the Ministry of Pensions and National Insurance.

The book is the work of a distinguished Study Group of the Royal Institute of Public Administration.

GEORGE ALLEN AND UNWIN LTD